Dr Harry Cooper's love for animals began when he was a young child. He studied veterinary science at Sydney University, and for the past 35 years has practised as a vet in Sydney, England and Tasmania.

Dr Harry joined 'Burke's Backyard' in 1987 and in 1993 became host of 'Talk to the Animals' on the Seven Network. In 1998 he filmed the first series of 'Harry's Practice', now about to enter its fourth year.

Dr Harry Cooper lives on a picturesque property in Relbia, in northern Tasmania, with his wife, Janine, daughter, Heidi, and an extended family of four-footed and winged creatures, including 27 horses, 12 dogs, 32 cats, 13 ducks and 8 rabbits.

DR HARRY COOPER

Anecdotes & Antidotes

MACMILLAN
Pan Macmillan Australia

First published 2000 in Macmillan by Pan Macmillan Australia Pty Limited
St Martins Tower, 31 Market Street, Sydney

Reprinted 2000 (twice)

National Library of Australia
cataloguing-in-publication data:

Cooper, Harry, 1944– .
Anecdotes and antidotes.
ISBN 0 7329 1024 2.

1. Cooper, Harry, 1944– – Anecdotes.
2. Veterinarians – Australia – Anecdotes.
3. Veterinarians – Australia – Biography.
I. Title.

626.089092

Illustrations by Elliot Cowan

Typeset in Sabon 12/16 by Midland Typesetters
Printed in Australia by McPherson's Printing Group

*For my human and my animal family,
and my best mate, Rosie.*

Contents

SADDLING UP

REAL BUSHIES

TALKING WITH THE ANIMALS

TV HOUSE CALLS

Introduction

Animals have been a part of our lives since the very beginnings of civilisation. They are for us an amusement, a crutch, an entertainment, a protection, a sport and a hobby. But above all else for me they are my constant companions and my friends.

For over thirty years I've practised as a vet both in Australia and England. I have met some wonderful people and some terrific animals. Many times I've thought that these encounters should be recorded so that people other than my friends and my family can enjoy them too.

What I've assembled here is just a small cross-section of those stories. In most cases the places and names are correct. Where I have omitted these I have done so to protect the privacy of the people concerned. All the stories are true. They all happened just the way I describe them.

Fortunately my family in Tasmania is animal mad too, for without their support my career in both television and veterinary practice could not be possible. Who looks after the farm when you're away? It's a big task and it's well done.

I hope that through my words you will experience just some of the special moments I have been privileged to enjoy. My wife Janine will tell you 'an animal's love is unconditional—people let you down but animals never do'. And it is my hope that those of our younger generation who live with and love their animals will take that love and the responsibility that goes with it into their adulthood so that they may carry on where I've left off. I hope too that having that respect and understanding for the animals of this earth will allow them respect and understanding for their fellow man.

Dr Harry Cooper
Relbia, Tasmania

A Bird Man
From Way Back

1

I've Got Budgies

I've been breeding budgies ever since I was a kid. And over the years I've had a disaster or two.

One happened about the time I moved from primary to secondary school. I'd spent my early years at a little private school in Hunters Hill. It was a truly beautiful place called 'Malvern', set on a huge block with a lovely old sandstone house and two wooden classrooms that held composite classes of grades one and two, three and four, five and six.

The headmaster was a man called Martin—well that was his surname; we all used to call him 'Sir'. He was a big tall man, the sort of guy that you really respected. He would wield the cane when he thought it necessary, but apart from teaching the rudiments of maths, English, geography and history he also engendered in all his pupils a real feeling of school spirit.

I loved that little school. I doubt that there were more than a hundred kids in the whole shebang. It had a great school motto, a wonderful school song, most of which I can still remember, and I'd look forward to the end-of-year athletics carnival and prize giving. We always had an official program and it was great to walk up those long stone steps to the front door of the house and receive your award for the year's work. It was a beautiful time of year. The jacarandas were in bloom and the whole area with its gravel driveway, sandstone staircase and wrought-iron adornments were all covered with a purple carpet of flowers. Year six was a good one for me. I was Dux of the school and first in the seventy-five metres sprint (I've put on a few pounds since then).

My dad was not all that flush with money, but he was determined to do the very best he could for my brother and me. To gain entry to the high school he had in mind I had to sit an entrance exam. Can you imagine a kid coming from a class of less than twenty and being thrust into a huge hall where nearly two hundred students were seated at desks, all striving for the same objective. Suddenly I wasn't H. L. Cooper, I was a number. It was stuck on me and was all over my examination papers. Three hours we spent in there. I was shell-shocked at the end of it.

My father always believed in the incentive reward scheme, much the same way most of us advocate training our dogs. He told me that if I was good enough to get into the school and get a scholarship as well then he'd buy me some budgies. Well, I was, and he did just that. He always was a man of his word, and that's one of the things I remember most about him. That, and his tremendous love for animals.

You can't imagine how excited I was. Two pair of birds. We installed them in some primitive cages in our fernery, right underneath my bedroom window. The cages were all wire contraptions, wonderfully old-fashioned looking things by today's standards, and the sort of thing Dad had used for breeding canaries in the past. In fact Dad had bred just about everything imaginable over the years: Fox Terriers, with his prefix 'Arcadian' (and after which our farm in Tassie is now called); Yorkshire and Roller canaries, both of which are pretty much a rarity today; Muscovy ducks; fantail pigeons; and he even had an interest in greyhounds as well as what in the older days were called the ponies (horses designed to race over just a quarter of a mile).

The budgies however needed a different set-up. They nest in boxes, not in open saucer-like devices, as do canaries. Still we managed to make things work, and the budgies knew what to do anyway. They bred like flies, or perhaps I should say mice. At any rate they bred and churned out chicks by the nestful— anything up to six in a clutch.

Have you ever seen a baby budgie? When they first hatch they have not one feather on them. My wife Janine reckons they always remind her of pink jelly babies. It takes a good week before you start to see any feathers at all. Mine were tiny little things, certainly by today's standards for exhibition budgies. They were mostly of a dirty yellow colour, and only half the substance of their modern-day cousins. But it was happening. Two birds mating, one laying eggs, after twenty days or so the hatching, then the rearing. It was incredible the way in which the hen bird managed to feed the youngest baby in the nest first and the oldest last. You see, the eggs are laid every second day so they hatch in the same sequence and the newest chick needs a different type of food to the oldest. It's called crop milk, which the hen bird (the female) produces in her proventriculus (that's the bird's equivalent to our stomach) and then she regurgitates this back to the chicks in a carefully measured amount.

Being able to breed something for the first time—other than silkworms of course—is a fantastic thrill. It is mother nature at work, and it's happening right in front of your eyes. So there were the chicks, sitting on the perch nervously at first and then proudly alongside Mum and Dad and looking for all the world just like them. It is the greatest education in the world. Somehow something that's alive will always have a far greater appeal to me than something that's purely materialistic. And nothing will ever give a greater thrill than to see a new creature come into the world. Whether it is by my hands or purely through a natural process in which case I am nothing more than a humble observer, the creation of a new being is something special, and something that man has only very recently learnt to duplicate, cloning. The amazing procedure that takes one tiny cell from a male and one from a female, blends them together, and lets them grow and finally develop to form a replica of one or the other parent is just a fantastic phenomenon.

All my mates caught the bug and they too went out and bought some birds. Suddenly there was a heap of us all breeding budgies and having a genuinely good time.

The hobby was a great one. We never seemed to be lost for things to do. We visited one another's homes and talked about our birds. And the birds did things, simply because they were alive. What's more they depended on us to look after them. They had to be fed, watered, and housed correctly. There was the need to add extra things to the diet when they were feeding their chicks. It taught us all a lot and the most important lesson was simply that of responsibility. We were responsible for their welfare and as kids that was a very important lesson.

My mum was pretty health conscious, so every Christmas holidays, without fail, my brother and I had our regular visit to the dentist. Lots of things puzzle me about dentists, but two in particular. First, I want to know where all the goldfish that used to live in dentists' waiting rooms have gone? If you are as old as me you'll remember that every dental waiting room always had the mandatory fish tank, with two or three orange fish swimming slowly backwards and forwards between the greenery. Have they been flushed down the toilet? Made redundant in favour of some electronic device? Fair dinkum, nothing could have the hypnotic effect of goldfish swimming back and forth. They almost subdued you before you entered the dreaded room of torture.

Point number two. Dentists never talk to you until they've stuffed your mouth full of cotton wool. So there I was seated in the chair gripping the arms with a vice-like tension, determined not to display any of my all too obvious fear.

'What have you been doing during the holidays?' the dentist asked.

'Oi ... gut ... udgis,' I struggled to reply.

'Oh, you've got budgies,' he said.

It strikes me that over the years dentists somehow have been able to translate the average Australian drawl that masquerades as language, even after it's been filtered through several centimetres of cotton wool and spoken with a mouth so dry that you can relive with terrible empathy the last hours of Burke and Wills as they died of thirst in Australia's interior, and still make sense of it all.

'I'll have to show you some good budgies,' he went on.

'Oi ... gut ... ood ... udgis,' I stammered out.

I mean to say, fancy insulting a thirteen-year-old kid by telling him his budgies are second-rate.

Nevertheless, the dentist did organise for me to see some of these good budgies. It turned out that Ken Caisley was a founding member of the Budgerigar Society of Australasia. Some two weeks later we pulled up outside a house in Five Dock. From the outside it was nothing special, just an ordinary home on an ordinary block in a fairly old suburb of Sydney. As we walked down the drive and into the backyard I could hear the birds already. But I wasn't prepared for what I was about to see.

There were at least two aviaries set against the back fence, not all that big, probably only two and a half metres long and about the same deep. Both had an open wire front, and were crammed so full of birds that there were always two or three in midair, hoping that a couple of others would take off so that they could find somewhere to perch. It's hard to estimate, and after all it was over forty years ago, but I'd guess that perhaps there were four or five hundred birds altogether. But it was the colour, that fantastic colour, that got me. Set against the white-painted aviaries it was just so unbelievable. I had never seen anything like it before and I've never seen anything like it since. Even after all this time I can still picture that afternoon so clearly. These birds belonged to a great breeder by the name of Harley Yardley, and if the name sounds familiar then you are correct—cosmetics were his business. Sadly, I never got to meet the man. He had passed away some few weeks earlier.

Today, we call these birds 'clear wings'. In those days I called them absolutely sensational. They were vivid green birds with golden wings or brilliant blues and purples with snow-white wings. Not a trace of black markings anywhere. Golly, I took one look and in a split second I knew this was the hobby for me—and it has been for most of my life. The great thing forty years ago about breeding birds of any description, be they budgerigars, canaries, finches, pigeons or poultry, was that there were lots of mentors. Today I think they are pretty scarce on the ground, and I'm not talking just about the bird world; I mean everywhere.

My dad was a great bloke and thought nothing of giving up a day every weekend or so to cart me around to different aviaries in Sydney. I had mentors all over Sydney, from Castle Hill to Caringbah, but somehow Dad didn't seem to care. These were great guys who had all the time in the world for young blokes like me. Their knowledge was the sort that only comes with experience, not the kind of stuff you pull out of books. Anyone with a good memory can commit that sort of material to the grey matter. I mean stuff learnt over many months watching, understanding and remembering. It's a shame that so much of it was never written down. Today we seem to be so busy we've lost the real art of learning by observation. Sometimes people in the city can look but they don't really see. There isn't the time to analyse or even imagine what is going on in front of their very eyes. I often think that our early pioneers in the sheep industry made more progress in the first one hundred years than we've made since. Somehow technology will never really replace the art of being a good observer.

These guys had a tonne of patience and I guess they needed it to deal with a young bloke who was just so exuberant about his new-found hobby. They helped in many ways: advice, demonstrations and giving me the odd bird as well. I joined the Budgerigar Society and met up with another young bloke just as keen and only a year or two younger than me. His first name was Don and his second name was Burke. He lived at Lindfield on the North Shore line and I lived at Lane Cove on the banks of the river with a view of the Harbour Bridge. The two of us shared many wonderful times with our fabulous hobby. In school holidays we spent days and nights at one another's homes. Our respective parents would cart us backwards and forwards to one another's places and we'd live, breathe and talk birds all day.

Don was particularly interested in crested budgerigars. He had quite a few. But the difficulty in breeding these birds was the unpredictability of the crest inheritance. By this stage I'd started at university and was developing a keen interest in genetics. Don kept very good records and we sat down one weekend to try and work out just how this particular mutation was inherited. It struck both of us that just perhaps it may follow the same pattern as the comb in poultry. You see, chooks—or poultry I should say—have different types of combs, such as Rose, Single, Walnut or Pea. And the pattern of their inheritance was well documented.

Over many hours and many sheets of paper we worked it out. No computers in those days—just pencils and rubbers. The pattern was the same. It fitted the records exactly. We wrote an article and sent it overseas to our favourite bird magazine, considered to be the 'Bible' of the bird world. The article was never published and we found out some years later that the then editor had contacted the head of our Society in Sydney to check on our credentials, only to be told we were just a couple of kids and didn't know what we were talking about.

Funny thing though, about two years later, our article appeared, almost verbatim, in the same magazine. Only trouble was it had someone else's name underneath it. He was a professorial type who'd spent much of his time researching bird diseases and writing on genetics. He never did get his research anywhere near right, always barking up the wrong tree—but then that's ancient history.

♦

We each went our own way—Don into horticulture and I into veterinary practice—and time moved on, as it has a habit of doing. We were not to meet again for many years, but that's a different story. I'd been married for about four years and we'd bought a house in Annangrove, in the Hills District to the west of Sydney. We'd spent two years in England working around the countryside and had come home looking for somewhere out of Sydney where we could have a bit of land and enjoy a semi-rural lifestyle—a place you'd like to raise a family. Somehow the places were either too big and too expensive or cheap enough but falling down. Eventually we found it. The place was perfect, set well back off the road, with a long drive-way on an even longer block that finished in the bush with a steep drop to the creek below. Eight acres in all, or three and a bit hectares. We made an offer and twelve hours before we were to sign the contract they pulled it off the market. Devastation is the only word you could use to describe the way we felt. We spent another six months looking and finally, after giving up on our acreage, we decided on a house in Carling-ford. You wouldn't believe it, 23 December, the day before we were to sign the purchase contract for the Carlingford property, the Annangrove house with its grassy acres came back on the market. Real estate is a dirty game, and trying to arrange any sort of finance around the holiday period is a real hassle. We stalled, we excused, until finally we got everything sorted out, ditched Carlingford and bought Annangrove.

Aviaries and dog kennels were built. I've still got 'birds eyes' on my knees from concreting the aviary floor. They were all well built with bricks and aluminium windows. Problem was, the first aviary simply blew away! You'd better believe it—and with no help from the birds, I can assure you. The aviary was in two parts; the bird room at the back, where all the breeding took place, was separated from the flying area in front by a fibro wall. The flight area in front just wasn't anchored down well enough. It faced north-west and one day a big willy-willy came through and the whole structure became airborne and ended up in the next-door neighbour's paddock, some twenty-five metres away. There were yellow budgies all over the Hills District—well at least fifty or so. I got very few back, but luckily the majority of the birds were still down at my parents' home. A good carpenter solved the problem and a solid wooden structure took the place of the flimsy pipe and fibre-glass forerunner.

I've bred a lot of budgies over the years, up to a thousand in a season. And that's from a hundred breeding boxes. There were birds everywhere, and it was quite a job looking after the whole concern, and keeping the records straight. On top of this, I was pretty heavily involved in the running of shows as well.

Every year on the holiday weekend in January the Budgerigar Society holds its annual show in Sydney. We were at Rose Bay, this particular year, at the R.S.L. Club, a great set-up with nearly one thousand birds to be judged. The day was a swine. It was stinking hot with a howling nor'-westerly screaming across New South Wales. There were bushfires everywhere. But somehow you never think that it could be your turn. Lunch was at about 12.30 p.m. and it wasn't long after that I got the message. A big fire was racing up the gully behind our house. It was totally out of control and I'd better get back just as soon as I could. No-one was home. Our first child was due in about ten days and my wife was with her parents, totally unaware of the drama that was about to engulf us all. I jumped into the trusty Valiant and was gone in a flash.

Our street was littered with the bright orange trucks of the Volunteer Bush Fire Brigades and through the smoke haze all you could see were the blackened fingers of the trees and the shrubs that only an hour or two earlier had been living breathing things. Now stark and dead in a landscape that was almost entirely black, as if designed by some force that never knew the very life that colour engenders. The wind was fairly howling out of the north-west, the sort of wind that I learnt to dread over the years. It was hot to start with, but got all the hotter as it fanned the flames of destruction on that terrible day.

I counted eleven houses burnt to the ground. The fire was well past our place and racing towards the North Shore. With a sort of frantic determination to get home, I fought my way along the familiar road now cluttered with ghoulish sightseers, weary blackened fire fighters and mindless onlookers. What is it about these people that seem to derive some sense of pleasure or enjoyment from the misfortune of others? The human race sure has a lot to learn from the animal kingdom.

I turned into the drive. Will the house still be there? What about the animals? A million questions, all without answers, whirled around in my brain. The front paddock was green and intact. I'd watered it all through the summer; it was probably the only green thing for miles around. The cows and the goats had survived. Everywhere else was just a blackened ruin. Everything was gone. No fences, no grass, no trees, no garden, nothing.

The house was still standing however, and appeared to be unscathed. But then smoke started billowing from the back. The verandah posts were alight. There was a mad scramble to grab a bucket and bale some water out of the old bathtub near the back door to put out the flames. Thank God for that, I quietly breathed. It was no good turning on the power; all the lines were down and some of the poles too. No water either. That's the first thing that goes. When I reckoned the house was secure and everything around it was hunky dory it was time to check on the livestock. It was not a pretty sight. I'd lost a lot of my greyhounds, either burnt or overcome by smoke and heat, although some did survive. It had all happened just too quickly and my neighbour's valiant attempts to let them out had been stifled by the very heat of the fire front. What a terrible death. I felt for every one of them.

All the poultry were gone. I'd been breeding Rose Comb bantams for a few years and had some really nice ones. They were getting ready for the upcoming shows. They have what we call large white lobes on the sides of their heads, which need to be protected as they sunburn very easily, so I'd kept them in wire cages covered with aluminium roofing to keep off the sun. Each cage housed just one bird and there were about a dozen or more. They had a glass jam jar wired in the corner for water, and a metal dish for food. There was just nothing left in any of the cages, no bones, nothing. Even the glass jars had melted and dripped through the wire floor onto the ground. In places the roofing had melted too. I believe aluminium melts at around 400 degrees C so that gives you an idea of the intensity of the fire.

The geese couldn't be found, not a sign of them anywhere. Then—I don't know what made me do it—I bent over and looked inside a forty-four-gallon drum that was lying on its side, near what remained of the primitive cattle yards which by now were nothing more than a pile of smouldering timber.

I used my left hand to steady myself as I bent over. There, huddled inside, were three frightened birds. What a pathetic sight. The poor creatures just couldn't comprehend what was going on around them. You have to feel sorry for animals when they show genuine fear and these birds were terrified. Feet, feathers and beaks were all so badly burnt. I got blisters on the palm of my hand from the outside of the drum, even all this time after the fire had passed. I threw a bucket of water over the poor devils and chased them out of their shelter. If only it would rain.

What about my precious budgies? I feared the worst and I was right. Nothing in the flights had survived. Four hundred and ninety-eight birds had died. They littered the floor or clung to the wire, choked by smoke or cooked by the heat of that terrible afternoon. However, something had made me shut the double doors on the front of the bird room that morning. In the summer they were usually open to allow a bit of circulation, but not this day. Inside the breeding room two hundred had survived. They were my second-best. Twenty years of breeding had gone up in smoke—or choked on it. I just couldn't look at them. I walked back to the house.

How do you handle something like this? You know you just have to. In hindsight we were lucky. The house was still standing and we still had all the material things we valued. To me though, somehow this all seemed very empty.

Soon after my wife and her family arrived and the clean-up began. We cremated what was dead—there was no shortage of funeral pyres—and tried to treat what was living. Everything that was still breathing was coughing. The air was still full of smoke, the wind continued to howl, and the roar of hollow trees gasping their last despairing breath was interrupted only by the crash of one already consumed by the blaze.

Since our front paddock was about the only bit of green grass in the whole area, by the end of the afternoon we had just about every horse, cow, sheep, or goat in the district ensconced in it. There were no fences intact anywhere, and this was the only safe haven for animals in the immediate vicinity. Any wandering livestock of any description was ushered into our top paddock. It was standing room only, and all the animals looked just so lost and bewildered by the whole experience.

It was a pretty sad afternoon, a matter of burning things that we couldn't repair and cleaning up as much as we could. Incredible things happened. To walk around and see dry lumps of cow manure sitting in the middle of a paddock with no fire anywhere near them suddenly burst into flames and burn is something quite frightening.

The heat was still unbelievable. The rains came, but if they hadn't it's a pretty fair bet that nothing would have stopped the fire that day until it got to the harbour, such was the force of the wind and the intensity of the heat.

At about eight o'clock the next morning as I lay in bed, not really wanting to get up, I thought I heard a car pull up at the side of the house. Then another one and another. I looked out the window and could see little but then glanced at someone walking down to the aviary with a broom.

Twelve of my friends from the bird world had turned up. Not members of my own club, but of a neighbouring one. Everyone in what we affectionately call the bird game knew what had happened; the grapevine was a pretty thriving one.

They worked most of the morning, these guys. Cleaning, sweeping and trying as much as possible to restore some sort of order in the shemozzle, and some sort of spirit to me. The aviary itself was intact but it was so quiet and so empty. They'd each brought with them a couple of birds and once the joint was cleaned, they released them into the flights. You've no idea how good it felt to see those birds flying again. Suddenly there was noise where there had been none and colour where only blackened walls had survived. Over the next few weeks and months birds arrived from everywhere. I'd get home and there'd be a box on the back verandah. Or a letter to tell me to pick up a parcel from the airport. Birds just kept coming. Most without even a note, from I knew not where and I knew not who. Sometimes a message scrawled on the box—'thought you could use them', 'your old line'—said enough.

People were fantastic. For some reason the camaraderie of the bird world is something special. I don't really know how to explain it, only that there is something different about people who breed birds. Perhaps it is that they share that love of the third dimension that only our avian friends can enjoy, the power to rise above the things on earth, the ability to leave troubles behind and fly! In our life together Janine and I have bred many different animals, horses, dogs, and cats to name a few. But in all these hobbies we've never experienced the same mateship as we have in the bird game.

This was all some twenty-five years ago, and only a matter of days before my daughter Tiffany was born. I got going again and continued to enjoy the hobby until we moved to Tasmania in 1988. I saw our annual shows grow to nearly two thousand entries. I saw the unification of all the states in a now centralised body. I've judged in most places. The budgerigar world came of age and I like to think that I helped in some small way. Birds are still a part of my life, even though I haven't bred a young'n for nearly ten years. It's in the bird game that I still have so many good friends, and they are friends for life. Now my days in telly are just too busy. It wouldn't be fair on the birds. They need my time—and in time, there will be time. I'll be back. Breeding birds is a bit like a drug; I'm hooked, and I'll admit it.

2

Bigger than Ben Hur

In veterinary practice birds had always been one of my speciⁱ-
alities. Right from the time I started university in Sydney I had
been determined to find out just as much about their medical
problems as I could. I even went as far as writing my final year
essay on the diseases of cagebirds. Back in those days—and I'm
talking nearly thirty-five years ago—very little was known.
And to be quite honest, even our lecturers seemed totally dis-
interested. Rather than deter me I considered it a challenge.

Most of the research had been done on chickens and it
became a matter of trying to transpose the dosage of a drug
that was meant for a flock of five thousand or so laying hens,
down to a level that would treat one budgerigar weighing
around seventy grams. It wasn't easy, but then most things
aren't when you first start out. Over the years more and more
of my colleagues became interested. Research began not only
here but in the United States and England where many of our
common parrots were worth so much more. Our knowledge
grew and with it we shed the 'Bird Man of Alcatraz' image—
and thank heaven for that. Medicines became available to treat
individual birds; anaesthetics improved, as did surgery, so we
could now operate quite safely on birds just as we had done on
dogs and cats.

♦

I got a call one afternoon from a long-term client of mine. She'd been given a pair of Sulphur-crested Cockatoos as a wedding present, and was a bit perplexed by the behaviour of one of the birds. She explained over the phone that every time the female sidled along the perch and started gently caressing the neck of the male, this funny pink thing would suddenly appear out of his rear end. It sounded interesting—very, very interesting. So I made an appointment for later on the next evening.

This young lady had been to see me on many occasions with a male Eclectus parrot that she kept as a pet. He was a great bird, probably not as attractive as the female of the species, but somewhat tamer. The male is a brilliant green nearly all over, with very little other colour, except a bright orange beak. The female, on the other hand, is a striking dark blue and red. It's quite the opposite to what you see in most birds, where the cock, or male bird, tends to be dressed more extravagantly than his female companion. This bird was really tame, could talk quite well and travelled around in the car sitting on my client's shoulder. She'd done such a good job with him I was sure she'd have no trouble with the cockatoos at all. But I wondered about this new-found husband of hers. I hadn't met him and perhaps he may not have the same way with birds that she had. Anyhow, time would tell.

Believing in discretion I made sure she had the last appointment for the evening, and she arrived with her new husband and the birds in their cage. For a change I seemed to be running on time and they didn't have to wait long before I got to see them. In they came and popped the cage up on the table. I was introduced to the new husband and quite probably they were the only words we exchanged during the entire consultation.

The three of us sat there watching the two birds, who seemed totally oblivious to our attention. They were caged in what was quite a large, solidly built wire cage—one of the newer models, the sort of thing you would see in most American bird magazines and yet rarely encounter back home, being almost twice the size of the normal cockatoo cage. I was assured that they spent most of their time either out of the cage roaming around the house, or outside in a large aviary, that filled something like half the backyard.

I reckon it only took five minutes before we saw some action. Sure enough the female crept slowly along the perch towards the male. In no time at all she was ruffling the feathers on the back of his neck. They did look a grand pair. Both birds were in top condition, with sleek plumage and bright eyes. No telltale signs of sickness here. Now, at this particular stage, it became apparent that my client's husband was not feeling 100 per cent comfortable. He took himself off into the corner of my consulting room. I should explain that the room is fairly small and apart from the table and a small area in one corner housing the sink and a desk, there's not much there at all. The whole thing is painted a bright yellow, the benches are white with red knobs on the cupboard doors. It looks pretty bright and it's easy to keep clean. There was obviously something out of place in this particular corner because for almost the entire consultation he stood there staring at it. Now I might tell you that I worked in that room for nearly ten years and on many occasions I've closely examined this particular corner and to this day I've never been able to find what was so fascinating about this particular area of the wall. But there had to be something because he never took his eyes off it for almost the entire visit.

It didn't take long for things to get underway. The female

kept on ruffling those neck feathers of his until, quite slowly at first, a somewhat thin pink object started to appear at the rear end of the male. It was difficult to make out at first with all those feathers in the way but, sure enough, the more amorous she became the more this pink thing started to grow in length and breadth and began to descend towards the floor of the cage. It got longer and longer, thicker and thinner, and moved in some peculiar sort of rhythmic contortion.

'Good 'eavens,' I said. 'It's big.'

'It gets bigger,' the young lady said.

'Strike me. It's bigger than Ben Hur. What happens when it touches the ground?'

'Well,' she said, 'it bounces up and down.'

Sure enough it did. The darn thing was half as long again as the bird and had now gone into this mysterious bouncing routine every time it touched the floor of the cage.

I had totally forgotten about the poor husband and I'm pretty certain that with all the goings on his new wife had forgotten about him too. After all it's not every day you get to see a male cockatoo with this huge, flesh-coloured strand of lithe pasta swinging merrily from its nether regions. The poor husband hadn't even moved since he first took up station in the corner. He kept staring, never taking his eyes off whatever it was that had him riveted to the spot—that is, until I disrupted his concentration by opening a drawer under the desk, right alongside where he was standing.

I pulled out a fairly large and gruesome looking pair of artery forceps, the instruments that we use to grab hold of a bleeding artery or vein during surgery to stop the bleeding until we get a ligature around the area. I opened and closed them several times just to make sure their grip was secure and they moved freely. They make a very mechanical sound when you do this and suddenly the new husband became interested in the proceedings. He watched over his shoulder as I opened and closed them several more times. I crossed the floor to the cage on the bench and slid open the door in the front. It was then that he threw a glance over his shoulder—to the cage, the birds, to his wife, to me, and in particular to the instrument that now rested firmly in my right hand. I reached inside and grasped the pink gyrating object with the business end of the forceps and squeezed them closed around the upper part of its anatomy. Meanwhile the hen bird just kept on stroking those feathers and the male kept on soaking up all the attention, seemingly quite oblivious to what was going on underneath him. Not so the new husband. He fully turned around. All colour had drained from his face and he seemed to be breathing more quickly than normal. There was a quick step forward to perhaps offer some advice then, having thought the better of it, he retreated again to the corner. By now all his attention was on the pink thing that was within my grasp.

I gave a good tug and he winced. No, he did a lot more than that. I'm sure he gave a somewhat agonised groan. It came out in the forceps, almost half a metre of it, still kicking and struggling. I laid it out on the bench where he could see it plainly. Still it continued to dilate and contract. At times it was barely a couple of millimetres thick, and then it would broaden out to nearly half a centimetre. In all it was well over fifty centimetres long.

The husband went back to the corner again, having never uttered a word. He still seemed to be having trouble breathing; in fact he had even gone a bit whiter, if that was possible. Not so that wife of his. She was bubbling over with concern for her 'little baby boy' in the cage. In fact everyone seemed concerned except the birds and the vet. We were the only ones who knew what really had been going on.

You see, dear readers, tape worms in birds are enormously long while the male appendage in a cockatoo is barely two millimetres in length. Anyway, I wormed the birds, placated the husband, and to the best of my knowledge they all lived happily ever after.

3

A Tranquillising Brew

Quite some time ago, back in the days when I was a partner at Gladesville Animal Hospital, this particular client bred a lot of parrots. And I mean a lot of parrots. We are talking here in the many hundreds, not in the ones and twos. They were mainly small ones, like cockatiels and African lovebirds. You'd all be familiar with them, but there were some larger birds in the collection as well. With this number of birds in the backyard— and believe you me with all the aviaries he had there wasn't much spare backyard left—there was always a lot of uneaten seed lying around. This attracted a lot of our native birds and introduced species as well, who thought it was fair game to come along and enjoy the free picnic. In particular he had a bit of a problem with doves. They are nice, quiet little birds, not native to our shores but whose manner is such that they cause very little trouble about the place—except when they are there in their hundreds. There were almost as many freeloaders outside the cages as there were parrots inside.

Anyone in aviculture knows that wild birds do pose quite a health risk to birds that are kept in captivity, through internal and external parasites in particular. This includes things like worms and coccidia on the inside, and lice and mites on the outside. My client's set-up was such that he had a lot of large open flights—what we know today as suspended aviaries. These are quite big cages made entirely of wire with a minimal framework. They are held above the ground some metres or so on stilt-like legs and the birds are unable to make contact with the ground. All of this is designed to prevent the birds from picking up infections that may build up in the soil.

Only the very back part of these large enclosures was covered; the flight area in the front was totally open to the world, as were the sides and of course the bottom. The wild birds—attracted, of course, by the large amount of food that the parrots, who are fairly messy eaters, scattered outside their enclosures—would roost on his aviaries and, as gravity controls so much of what we and our animal friends do, their droppings would fall through the wire on the top and foul the wire on the sides or the bottom. In some cases the food and water receptacles became soiled by their excreta as well.

He'd tried lots of things to eliminate the problem. There were fake cats, there was bunting, there were electric wires and in some cases double layers of wire around the flights. All this did was to keep the birds of prey away; doves might look dumb but they weren't to be fooled by all of these man-made artifices. Everything he tried came to naught. There just had to be a simple solution.

We started trapping the doves and transporting them across to the other side of town. This was pretty simple. They would walk into any trap you like. They are so quiet and easy to handle they didn't get stressed at all. The trip across town took almost an hour in both directions. Trouble was the doves seemed to be reproducing at a faster rate than we could trap and transport the blighters, in my opinion because the babies were being reared on the best bird seed in town. I'll swear that some of them even found their way back to his backyard. After all, why wouldn't you return to the best restaurant in town, particularly when you don't have to pay the bill?

'Why can't we poison them?' he asked.

'Probably not a bad idea,' I thought. But poisoning wasn't what I had in mind. I wasn't at all keen on actually killing them.

I suggested we lace the seed with a tranquillising drug, catch them and transport the whole lot as far away as possible. The plans were laid and we impregnated a whole heap of wheat with a drug that would simply knock the birds out long enough for us to be able to round them up and get them into some cages, and transport them. We waited for the right afternoon: a lovely sunny day in the middle of summer. The birds would come down to feed at about four o'clock. An hour before, my client laid the bait. I wasn't actually there to witness the whole scenario. I was flat out at the clinic. So I can only relate what happened second-hand. Sure enough at four o'clock or a little thereafter the doves appeared in their hundreds. Perched on the roofs of the surrounding houses, they waited their time before alighting for afternoon tea. It didn't take long. They started their polite bowing and cooing to one another, and very soon they were taking a good crop full of the tranquillising brew. I reckoned it was going to take around twenty minutes before the drug would make them sleepy enough for him to catch. I was pretty right. Trouble was no-one told the birds.

It just so happens that my client's house was under a major flight path for Sydney airport. There were all the birds, merrily stuffing their insides, walking around, crooning to one another about what a great establishment this was, when suddenly into Mascot flew this massive aircraft. It came in low and loud. Someone said it was one of those huge Russian transport jobs. Anyhow, the damn thing made one horrendous din. The birds hadn't encountered anything quite like this before. It was noisier, bigger and lower than anything they were used to. The parrots went ballistic, and in a chain reaction the horde of doves took to the skies. Birds were going in every direction. The situation was suddenly totally out of control. They wheeled and circled above their favourite restaurant before coming to roost, somewhat unsteadily I'm told, once again on the neighbours' roofs.

It was about this time, its effects no doubt speeded up by the exercise, that the drug started to take effect. One by one the birds became a little drowsy. Somehow life seemed to be taking a turn for the worst, well at least a turn sideways. Their sense of balance deserted them. One by one they rolled down the roofs and into the gutters. And there they lay, out of reach and out of sight for the rest of the afternoon. I am often reminded of the saying, the best laid plans of mice and men often go astray. In this case I guess you could substitute birds for mice. There was no way of getting the birds out of the darn gutters. The few that did make it back down to the aviaries were rounded up in no time, but the majority of the freeloaders were now happily snoozing off the effects of my tranquilliser while lying belly up in the neighbouring roof drainage systems.

Now that would be the end of the story, but alas there is one more chapter. Those of you who have spent a hot February day in Sydney would know that on many afternoons the city is greeted by an almost mandatory thunderstorm. This hadn't figured in our calculations either. About two hours had passed when, in no time at all, the skies blackened, the lightning punctuated the darkness and 'Huey', the Aussie God of Rain, sent her down by the bucket-load. You can imagine what happened. The rain poured onto the roofs from where it cascaded down into the gutters.

Now a heavily tranquillised dove fits almost perfectly into the opening of a downpipe. Almost simultaneously, all the downpipes on all the roofs became blocked with snoozing doves. The result was disastrous. Water flowed everywhere but where it should've. Down walls, across ceilings—a minor catastrophe that affected some ten or more houses immediately surrounding my client. His house however escaped any damage because long before he had installed deterrent wires above his roof line.

Come morning the evidence was gone. The doves had awoken and flown off. One or two may have been lost—I mean how long can a dove hold its breath under water?—but I'm sure no-one was aware of what happened or why on that particular afternoon. No-one except the two of us—and I've never told anyone up until now. Suffice it to say that any more attempts at tranquillisation were abandoned and, discretion being the better part of valour, my client 'upped stakes' and moved to a more rural setting where the doves seemed less numerous and the roofs of his neighbours' houses were a good bit further away.

There has to be a moral in a story like this, and there certainly is. Never attempt to tranquillise animals in a situation where you don't have total control.

4

Duck Dive

A colleague of mine has a simple tale about tranquillisers. At the local golf course there were two quite substantial lakes, both of which were populated by several pairs of wild duck. The birds were everybody's favourites and when it came to the breeding season and the little fluffy ducklings were out on the water, well, you just had to stop in the middle of your round and contemplate mother nature and her handiwork for a moment or two.

One night, however, trouble struck. A pack of dogs got well and truly stuck into the flock and their babies, killing a good many and maiming one or two more. It's always a tragedy when this sort of thing happens. Dog packs are a problem in some semi-rural areas. Even though many of the dogs might be great family pets, when in a pack situation things change. It is then that they regress to more wolf-like behaviour and go out on these 'thrill kill' binges. Stricter dog control laws can't come soon enough for me—and let's hope they bring a greater sense of responsibility to any thoughtless owners.

Anyway, like the good vet that he is, my mate answered the call for help and was down at the golf course before surgery to see what could be done. Unfortunately he had to put down several badly injured birds. But there was one that couldn't fly although it could still walk. It obviously needed help. To catch it was the point.

These were wild birds, yes. But they were used to being fed, so he did just what I had done those years earlier and laced the food with a fairly hefty dose of a tranquilliser and sat back to see what would happen. Three of the remaining ducks came ashore as well as the injured survivor, and they all ate the medicated food. He hadn't thought of that one. But no worries, the drug would work in twenty minutes and he'd just cage them all up after treatment and let them sleep it off.

Some days you know from the moment you get out of bed that Murphy was definitely an optimist and everything that can go wrong most definitely will go wrong. The birds finished their tucker in no time at all and, being more than a little stressed by the action of the night before, decided that safety definitely lay out on the water not on dry land. Almost on cue, after twenty minutes the ducks began to behave differently. Their swimming became slower. And rather than proceeding in a straight line they started swimming in circles. Then the circles got smaller and smaller. Having lost their 'rudders' they now lost their sense of balance too and began rolling over in the water. It was hard to stay upright and it was rapidly becoming downright impossible.

Now an upside-down duck can't breathe. An upside-down duck drowns. It took my mate no more than ten seconds to make a decision. Thank heavens it was summer. Straight down to his undies he stripped and into the lake. There were eels and heavens knows what else in that murky water, but the only thing on his mind were the poor ducks. Like a real rescue at sea, one by one he grabbed the now stricken birds and holding them by their legs, well above his head, as the water was up to his armpits, he waded back to shore. Boy, did he stink!

They say 'all's well that ends well' and this ending was a

good one. All four survived and the injured duck, although never able to fly again, is now safe and secure inside a fence that protects both lakes. My mate tells me that even at the age of at least eight years she manages to produce a healthy clutch of chicks every season. Good old mother nature. She can use a hand occasionally and, you know, I think she's grateful for all our efforts.

5

Beauty, Power and Grace

Keeping waterfowl is a fascinating hobby. You need a lot of room and obviously you need some water. I had a client out Windsor way west of Sydney who was absolutely rapt in his birds. He had a fantastic collection, not just of ducks but of geese and swans as well. Some were pretty run-of-the-mill varieties but others were very expensive indeed.

Foxes can present quite a problem to anyone with poultry of any kind. But they seem particularly attracted to waterfowl, and when there are young cubs to feed, they can be very daring and even hunt during daylight hours.

I can well remember clearing some scrub down the back of the block in Annangrove and the ducks were out having a bit of a scavenge for insects where I'd been working. All animals love to investigate newly turned soil, and not just for worms and the like, but for the minerals and trace elements. I stopped to relax for a while, put down the mattock and strolled over to pick up the brush cutter again. Totally without warning and right in front of my eyes, this fox raced up no more than ten metres away, grabbed a duck around the neck and took off into the scrub. For a second or so I was paralysed. No-one expects this sort of thing, particularly with all the noise I was making. That fox had to be pretty darn hungry. But even so, nothing knocks my ducks off, certainly not in front of me. So I was off in hot pursuit, crashing and charging through the bush, brandishing a brush hook, yelling and screaming like a crazy idiot. With all the noise, it's a wonder that everyone for miles around didn't know I was hot on the trail of this four-legged furry thief.

'Stop, stop,' I yelled, as if the fox could understand. 'You rotten mongrel of a thing,' I shouted, as well as a few other words that I cannot commit to print. I couldn't see where it'd gone but just kept on running. Then, as if he or she had heard my commands, the culprit did just as I had asked and dropped the duck. She seemed fine. There was hardly a mark on her. And sure enough, when I carried her back to the rest of the flock, she simply waddled over and went on with the usual 'gidday, it's good to see yer' behaviour that is typical of Muscovies. You see, they don't quack and are probably more like geese than ducks. Somehow I don't think she realised she'd just had a close brush with death.

Now this client of mine that I mentioned before was well aware of the problem of foxes. He'd protected his dam and the five acres around it with chain wire fencing two metres high. It must have cost him a fortune but it was well and truly fox-proof—and that was the aim. The birds had free rein inside the enclosure and most were pinioned. This is a procedure which renders them unable to fly but affects nothing else. This technique is used by most waterfowl collectors right around the world and at many wildlife parks too. It's a very simple operation and is often performed on recently hatched ducklings at about three to five days of age. The idea is, of course, to keep the breeding pairs safe inside their compound and for them to have the ability to move wherever they want.

Since many of these birds were pretty pricey and it wouldn't have been possible to roof over such a huge area, pinioning was the only answer.

So when my client purchased a pair of mute swans, he asked if I'd be kind enough to do the same job on them. Whilst the operation on the babies is pretty straightforward—since they are small, easy to handle and there is virtually no bleeding—on adult birds a full anaesthetic is required to restrain the birds, and it becomes a much more delicate piece of surgery.

He dropped the birds in after surgery one night. They were huge, magnificent white creatures that could barely stand in the very large crates in which they'd arrived. I could only fit one in each hospital cage, that would normally house a greyhound. And they were strong too, very strong with an enormous wingspan. And darn big feet! I'd anaesthetised plenty of birds before but none as big as these two.

I could see by the diary that the next day was going to be flat out, so I reckoned on operating after my dinner that night, rather than try to squeeze them in and rush the job. Better to operate on a full stomach—and besides it was my favourite, roast lamb. About an hour or so later it was time to deal with my two patients. Now anaesthesia in birds has come a long, long way over the last fifteen years. Vets have so many great drugs and machines to make our job easier—and a lot safer for our patients as well. We use very few injections and rely almost entirely on gas. But to get these big swans to breathe that gas in, wasn't going to be easy. It took quite an effort to restrain them. The female was first. We held the mask over her face. The power in those wings and a neck that seemed to squirm in every direction made it hard to keep the gas going into the bird and not us. It took a good five or six minutes before the drug started to take effect. Slowly the struggling stopped and she became limper and limper. The flow of anaesthetic was adjusted and I was ready to go.

Surgery involves amputating the very tip of the bird's wing—just a couple of small bones really, and a few of the larger flight feathers. Then you need to tie off the blood vessels and suture the skin back in place. Once done properly it is hard for the average person to notice anything different. It took around ten minutes to do the job and I placed her back on the floor on a blanket to recover.

The male was even bigger and stronger than his girlfriend and she was still half asleep when I put him down alongside her to recover as well. Surgery on both had gone without a mishap, and I'd been very happy with the way they handled the anaesthetic. We cleaned up the few feathers and the instruments while the two of them lay side by side at my feet. As I bent down to check the wounds for any bleeding, they awoke with a start almost simultaneously. Both got to their feet, almost without effort, and stood for just a minute or so as if collecting their thoughts. Suddenly the male stood right up to his full height, stretching his neck high into the air in a defiant salute. With me kneeling on the floor, he was a good foot or so higher than me. I couldn't help it. Rocking back on my haunches, I just knelt there and watched him. This most majestic of all birds came straight up to me, snaked his head down to my face and then lifted his long neck high into the air, well above my head. Then he opened his wings to their full extent, beat the air three or four times with his outstretched plumage and looked down on me kneeling there as if I was paying homage to him!

Animals know how to do that. They know how to make you

feel humble. Like King Solomon's 'lilies of the fields and birds of the air' the Lord has given them a grace and beauty that with all our technology we can never hope to emulate. There is so much natural beauty in those feathers, so much power in those wings and so much grace in that body. What inferior beings we really are. The swan knew it—and so did I. There he stood, shining and glistening, a huge white angelic figure. Looking up I said to him, right out loud, 'you are the most beautiful thing I have ever seen.' He was, and still is, the most magnificent bird that has ever entered my surgery. As I spoke he turned away, called to his mate, and together they walked out of the room.

There have been many humbling experiences for me in veterinary practice: patients that have recovered in spite of my efforts, and not because of them; animals that have fought back from the grave; creatures so splendiferous that they defy description. But this, my friends, will live on as the most meaningful of all. That night it took a bird to teach me the lesson of humility, a swan who knew he was so much better than me in so many ways! I may have taken away a small part of one wing, but he'd experienced that third dimension that we earthbound humans cannot ever hope to encounter for ourselves. Birds fly and swans do it so well. Watch them when you have the chance. Stop, look, and then perhaps you'll understand the way I felt that night, and still feel today.

6

Dead Easy, Mate

Ever since I was a kid I'd been keen on poultry of some sort. It would have been very difficult not to be otherwise with a father like mine. In his time Dad had bred racing pigeons, Muscovy ducks and quite a collection of other poultry, including Buff Orpingtons and Australorps. To those of you who don't know much about the various breeds, a walk around any of the major agricultural shows next time you get a chance will open your eyes. The variety of birds is quite incredible, and the colours are just amazing. It's always been somewhat of a thorn in my side that backyard poultry keeping has become almost extinct through the action of those who think they know what's best for us. The sound of a cockerel crowing in the morning is not music to some people's ears but rather a vexation to the soul. Oh, you poor lifeless people! Animals are the very thing that help to bring stability to our lives. It's a pity that children miss out on the chance to grow up with such a simple hobby as poultry keeping; it costs so little and its rewards are so great. So much for progress. No wonder our stress levels start to peak before we even become teenagers!

Back at Annangrove I had quite a collection of poultry. I was really keen on Rose Comb bantams and the bigger version of the same bird called Hamburgs. They were a very neat, compact bird. I had them in black, white, silver-spangled and gold-pencilled. They were pretty too, beautifully coloured. Their combs were their crowning glory. Very unlike what you see on most poultry, they were broad at the front and sort of crinkly on top, very much like a chocolate bar with bits of nut sprinkled throughout. They were bright red in colour, and tapered to a point at the back like a pencil which projected out and away from the head. Their other dominant feature was their two lobes. These are probably better thought of as earlobes and in this breed they were large, white areas of featherless skin that lay just below and slightly behind the eyes. The contrast between the black feathers, the bright red comb and these strikingly white lobes was what made the breed one of my favourites.

The trick with these poultry is to not only breed birds with good overall confirmation but to have good comb quality and uniform feather markings as well. My birds ran in quite a large flock at the rear of the property, together with a few silky bantam crosses. These little old ladies with feathers growing just about everywhere on their bodies, including their legs, were really great foster mothers. Their matronly instincts seemed always to be to the fore, which made them almost continually broody. They would sit on just about anything, including china eggs. One even sat on a 'clutch' of golf balls whilst waiting for a batch of the genuine article to foster. I could settle a good dozen or more eggs underneath them knowing they'd hatch them out and rear the chicks without a worry. All except the stock that I had set aside for specific breeding, lived in the open communal run. Here the silkies brooded and reared their chickens, the young Rose Combs grew and developed, and the spare breeding stock did their best to keep up a constant supply of small but neat, white eggs.

As always, foxes were a real headache, so I made sure all the birds were locked up in their run before sunset every night. The eggs, of course, were always useful, and the neighbours would drop in from time to time for some free-range 'cackleberries'.

Suddenly egg production seemed to plummet. On top of that I began to lose one or two small chickens. Must be crows, I figured. There were plenty of the mongrels around and quite frankly I've never liked the damn things. Their mournful cry and the cruel damage they inflict on sheep and the lambs while the poor ewe is attempting to give birth makes them not just a scavenger but a predator. On top of that they have a reputation for stealing eggs, golf balls, and anything that even looks like an egg. It didn't take a genius to figure the easiest way to fix that problem was to cover the whole of the yard with some nylon netting. The stuff they use for prawning seemed to be the go and the local fish markets had a plentiful supply. With that fixed over the yard I figured my problems were over. Dead wrong!

I just couldn't work out what was happening. From getting fifteen to twenty eggs a day I was suddenly down to two or three. And what's more, one of the sitting silkies seemed to have lost half her eggs as well. Gotta be the kids next door, I reckoned. So instead of letting the birds out to free-range during the day, I kept the door of the yard shut and locked it as well since it was almost impossible to keep the pen under observation from the house. The Annangrove property was something like eight acres altogether, a long skinny block and the poultry was some one hundred and fifty metres from the house. Not only that, there was an orchard in between as well. Well, that certainly did stop things and soon production was back to normal. I reckon it just had to be the kids, but for the sake of good neighbourly relations I shut up about it. The one rather confusing element in all this was that I never found any trace of broken eggs or eggshells lying anywhere around the place. Yep! It had to be the kids.

It was a Saturday afternoon and the poor birds hadn't been out for a pick for over a fortnight. Why not, I thought. I'm down here, I'll keep an eye out. They really enjoyed scratching around in the leaf litter looking for this and that. It's a natural thing for chooks to do. The whole area was surrounded by bush and there was plenty of scope for the hens to wander off and search here and there for an extra titbit to add to their diet. I wasn't paying too much attention, just straining up a couple of fences and trying to work out how the fencing contractor had made the whole procedure look so simple and here I'd been battling for something like forty minutes and hadn't even been able to get any tension on the darn apparatus at all. Suddenly World War Three broke out in the chook shed. There was the greatest cacophony you're ever likely to hear emanating from the tin shed. There was banging on the walls. Chooks and feathers were flying in every direction. Clouds of dust filled the air. It was like someone was being murdered. I sprinted for the door of the yard and slammed it shut.

'Gotcha ya mongrel, gotcha,' I yelled triumphantly. And out of the chook house marched this somewhat disturbed and very excited goanna. He was big, he was mean, and he wanted out of there, and out of there in a hurry. He made three or four hurried laps of the enclosure, as if working out some escape strategy and then flew up the wire. Goannas can climb like the wind. He pushed and shoved against the netting on top of the enclosure but it held firm. Down he came and had another go, all the time that big long tongue snaking in and out of a very mean-looking mouth. There was no way I was going in there without a bit of advice.

In my five years of veterinary school, I never remember receiving any lectures on how to handle an out-of-control goanna, or to give him (and we'll presume it was a him, because I never did get round to discovering just what sex it was) any sedation. This called for some expert advice. The thief was going nowhere but he was still trying. Up and down the wire, charging at the nylon netting which, thank heavens, held firm.

Henry Hirschorn was a mate of mine, a vet who specialised in all manner of reptiles. He practised down at Warriewood, a suburb on Sydney's northern beaches. A man with his sort of expertise would have just the answer to controlling this scoundrel. 'Henry ol' fella, I've got this mongrel goanna in my chook yard. How do I get hold of him?'

Now in veterinary practice we are often asked some fairly hairy questions, for it seems that possessing a veterinary degree empowers you to solve any and all manner of problems associated with any living creature, be it an elephant, a chihuahua or a goldfish.

'Dead easy, mate,' Henry said. 'Just walk up behind him and grab him with one hand behind his head and another around the top of his tail.'

'Cut it out, Henry,' I said. 'This bludger is over six feet long, and probably weighs sixty pounds.'

'Well,' he said, in his usual very relaxed fashion, 'better be careful of his claws while you're doing it.' Henry always understated things.

'You damn well come up and do it,' I thought. 'You're the expert.' But it was going to be up to yours truly to catch this lanky lizard.

In practice there just has to be an answer to most situations and it's just a matter of time before the penny drops. Eventually I devised a technique for catching the four-legged filcher. The shot was going to be grabbing him behind the back of the neck and then turning a hessian bag inside out over the top of him. Sounds dead easy, doesn't it? But once inside the yard the sight of this huge lizard rampaging all over the place convinced me that discretion was definitely the better part of valour. There was no way I was going to put my hands anywhere near this bloke.

The longer he stayed trapped in the yard the crankier he got. It was time for plan B. So instead of my hand I decided to use a noose which I'd slip over his head and around his neck. Sounds great in theory—but putting it into practice proved to be something else. This guy had read the manual on escapism. He could dart off in any of fifty directions just as soon as the rope, fixed to a pole, got anywhere near his head. I've got to tell you, the one thing that really terrified me was the thought of him shinning up my leg like it was a gum tree. I only had my 'stubbies' on.

Well, he won the first three rounds. The bell went for the next round and he made the mistake of heading back into the shed. Having gone in he had to come out. As he did I dropped the noose around his neck. Now the very thought of a goanna walking on a lead was foreign to both the lizard and myself, so quickly the bag was slid along the rope through a small hole in the bottom corner. It was a large potato sack, and when I thought the animal was quiet enough I whipped the bag inside out and over the top of the bludger. By now most of the sting had gone out of him. He thrashed around for a while and then settled down. The noose came off and the top of the bag was secured. Next question was what to do with the thief. He was really heavy and those claws could have ripped you apart. It's no wonder they can race up and down trees like they do.

I shouldn't have been too cranky, I suppose. After all, the natural diet for these guys does consist of eggs and small birds and mammals. It's just that he was using our chook shed as his regular restaurant, and what's more he never stayed long enough to pay the bill let alone leave a tip.

These beautiful reptiles are protected, so transportation to an area as far away as possible seemed to be the best bet. Down the Windsor Road, over the Hawkesbury River, and along the irrigated flats we drove. This seemed a good spot. I'd been driving for half an hour. We pulled into a country lane. I opened the passenger door and the top of the bag, hung the entrance outside, and waited. Quietly and sedately he crawled out and without even so much as a look behind him he changed gear into overdrive and charged off into the scrub.

There seemed to be a lot of weight still in the bag however, and I'd definitely only caught one lizard not two. So what was it that he left behind? Well my dear readers, this is the part of the story you're going to find hard to believe. Inside the sack were twenty-two eggs. They were all totally intact and most didn't even have a mark on them, not a scratch or even a puncture. He'd vomited up the lot on the journey from home. The majority of these he'd obviously taken from underneath my silkie foster mothers and just swallowed the lot whole. Talk about eat and run! So what do you do with twenty-two eggs that have spent the last hour or so in the belly of a very large goanna? They looked okay and still felt slightly warm—the whole episode hadn't actually taken all that long. So I did what any other good poultry keeper would do. I put them back where they came from. The little silkies seemed happy enough to have a nice lot of eggs to mollycoddle again, the rest of the fowlyard seemed to have settled down and life for the poultry at least seemed to have returned to normal.

The corollary—and yes there is a corollary—is simply this. Of the twenty-two eggs that seemingly had a second chance at life, twenty of them hatched.

7

A Bird in the Hand...

My dear old mum always told me, 'You start off in married life the way you mean to end.' Janine had learnt to accept that budgerigars had been and would always be a major part of my life. Every night after surgery I'd be down in the aviary, spending an hour or so checking through the nest boxes, slipping a ring or two on the legs of the youngsters, feeding a little green food here or there, and generally enjoying my hobby and unwinding after the strains of the day in the clinic.

You need some form of relaxation. It's something you have to do. A psychologist friend of mine described a hobby as a passionate diversion, which simply means throwing yourself into something completely different, but with the same vigour with which you enmesh yourself at work. He had a mate who used to come home from the office, get into a diving suit, with all the gear—weighted boots, helmet, hoses connected and pump going. He'd jump into the swimming pool, walk to the deep end, sit cross-legged on the floor and meditate for an hour. You've guessed it, he was a psychiatrist too. Maybe they're all mad.

For me, the budgerigars were my diversion and my sanity. I always changed clothes before going down to the aviary. Feathers, dust and droppings were not the sort of thing that were relished in the house, and invariably I'd leave my aviary clothes in a heap somewhere just inside the laundry. My then wife-to-be was a very tidy lady. Everything in the right place, and everything just right. They say you're attracted to opposites and nothing could be closer to the truth.

Our bedroom had a lovely aspect. It faced the north and the east and copped the sun nearly all day. We had a large area of slate on the floor immediately behind two huge glass sliding doors. The big yellow ball would beam down on the tiles and at night, with the curtains drawn, they would act like a large natural radiator. There was a spa in the bathroom off to the side and a huge walk-in wardrobe. Janine collects clothes like philatelists collect stamps so we needed the room, believe you me, we needed the room.

I think it was late one evening when my darling commented on a peculiar smell that seemed to be emanating from somewhere in the bedroom. Her schnoz was always better than mine, both in looks and sensitivity. Too many arguments with rugby goalposts had damaged mine beyond any reasonable olfactory activity, and the hookey bit in the middle, the result of a poorly set fracture, served mainly to stop the spectacles from falling off my face. Nevertheless, by the next day, even I could smell something just that little bit off in the atmosphere. Doors and windows were opened, the air freshener produced, and all seemed right with the world.

By that evening, however, the smell had become a stench. 'It's your bloody cats,' I said. 'One of them has snuck in here and pooped behind the cupboards.'

'No way, my cats don't do that sort of thing.'

Well we turned the place upside down. Looked behind all the cupboards, looked in all the corners, even looked inside the chest of drawers, and inside our shoes! Not a sign. 'Gotta be in the plumbing, I reckon.'

Next morning, the plumber arrives. Mission impossible begins. Every drain in the joint gets a thorough re-bore and disinfection. 'Not in the drains,' was the report from Keith my plumber. He's moved north since and given it all away, but the guy hated telling people he was a plumber and drainer, and always gave his profession as a 'hydraulic engineer'. Anyhow, back to the problem at hand, Janine then had me up in the ceiling, looking for dead animals. Possums or rats, heaven knows what. There was nothing except the skin off both knees from crawling around on the rafters for half an hour. And still the smell persisted. It even intensified. 'I've gotta get out of here,' Janine said.

I thought that a great opportunity to offer a nice night out at a local restaurant. A good feed, or a bunch of flowers, works wonders. Besides it's cheaper than a new dress. So we showered and changed.

It was then, that all was revealed. I'll admit it, right here and now. I and I alone was responsible for the terrible stench. You see one night, some ten or twelve days earlier, I'd done something I don't usually do. I'd streaked down to the aviary, after we'd come back from the movies, without changing. I was walking around checking the various aviaries when I came across a bird that was having severe trouble breathing. Really severe trouble. Lying on the floor feet up. Yes folks, it was dead. Now being the good vet that I am, or was, you never let this sort of thing happen without performing a detailed autopsy. Very often the death of one bird may mean the start of an epidemic. So I shoved the bird in my pocket and walked back to the house. I don't know what happened after that. Maybe it was the phone, maybe it was something else. Who knows, I'm easily distracted at the best of times, and it doesn't really matter anyway. But without thinking, I'd hung up my good pair of trousers in the wardrobe with the dead bird still in the pocket. Well there you go, now everyone knows I'll never live it down. The bird was removed and the trousers too, both to the garbage. It'll never happen again ... well, not until the next time, but what disappoints me is that I never did find out what it died from.

In Herriot's
Footsteps

8

Head Cow Man

Thirty years ago I was twenty-five years old, and my first wife and I decided to move to England. It was the era of 'Barry McKenzie' and his mates swigging on the 'frosty Foster's'. There were thousands of Australians living and working in England. Somehow the idea of being in central London, in 'Kangaroo Valley' so to speak, with all these Aussies and Kiwis was not the way I thought England and its customs should be appreciated. The country was the best option and, being a vet, finding jobs was not all that difficult.

To start with, a few weeks working in a lovely old village called Cheshunt, on the road to Cambridge, was just the thing to get the feel of practice in a totally new environment. Bruce Mallows owned the practice and he'd injured his back in an accident a day or too earlier. Could I do a week or so, the locum office enquired, while he recovered? No problem. You could get to the place by train so out I went for an interview. I got the job and borrowed the practice van to collect all our luggage from the London hotel.

It took something like four hours to complete a one-hour journey. I was dizzy from driving around roundabouts five or six times while we figured just which of the five exits was the right one. Bruce thought we'd stolen the van. But he and his wife became great friends and their house, an ancient two-storey home with a resident ghost, a past lord of the admiralty, became our base for the next two years. Every so often I'd pop back and work a week or two while he and his wife popped off for a well-earned break.

It was time for a move and other parts of the countryside were calling. A trip on the A30 heading in a west-south-westerly direction from London brings you to Salisbury, in the county of Wiltshire. A cathedral city, with a ton of history and a wealth of atmosphere, it is situated on a massive plain, far enough inland to be darn cold and open enough to the gales to be downright miserable. So that's of course where the British army was based and so were we.

It was Christmas Day. Salisbury was blanketed in a deep, cold, crisp layer of snow. We wanted a white Christmas, and by golly we had it. I'd been working in the practice for about a month or so and Jim Bruford, the boss, had invited us around to his home for Christmas lunch. It was just so different from an Australian Christmas, the sort of thing we'd only read about in books and seen on the front of Christmas cards. It was fantastic. We had all the trimmings. I was so full of food that it was hard to move. Jim and I sat in front of the fire enjoying a quiet tot of rum. And then, as it always does when you're a vet and feeling warm and relaxed, the phone rang.

It was a call to a nearby farm and a cow with milk fever. It's a pretty simple job. You just run in a bit of liquid calcium from a bottle; that reverses the problem, and up they get. Well usually. We drew straws to see who'd go. Jim drew the short one and I settled back in the chair.

No more than five minutes later the wretched phone rang again. Gee, I wish I'd drawn the short straw. On the phone was the head cow man from one of the local Lord's farms. The Lord owned a number of farms, each one controlled by an obviously superior being known to all as 'the head cow man'. Now if you think that serfdom was a thing of the past in the 1970s in southern England, then you'd be dead wrong. There was a massive pecking order established on all of these farms from the head cow man, right down to the bloke who washed off the shovel after the bloke in front of him had shovelled up you know what.

There he was, this fine specimen of a man, waiting at the front gate for my arrival. From a distance it was hard to tell who was holding up what. Both the gate and the head cow man were at a distinct angle to the vertical. I guess, though, as the gate had been there for some two or three hundred years, it was the one in the supporting role. The head cow man didn't paint a very pretty picture; his eyes conveyed his mental attitude—glazed. You know, the lights are on, but no-one is really home. Still, it was Christmas and he had been enjoying himself too.

'So, where's the cow?' I asked.

'On the pond, on the pond, laddie,' came the reply.

Now I have to explain at this juncture that the Poms don't have dams. They have lakes, and waters, and rivulets and streams but they don't have dams. Anything that holds still water is a pond. We walked on down the laneway, through the slush and slime that was a mixture of melting snow and cow manure, past the ancient brick and flint barns that were just so characteristic of the Salisbury area, turned the corner and there she was.

I find cows to be really nice animals. Most are fairly good looking and of fairly gentle disposition. But this poor, ungainly sod lay in the middle of the pond on a sheet of ice with each of her four legs aimed in the direction of the major points on the compass. She looked anything but composed, spread-eagled as she was on what must have been a pretty chilly resting place. Even from where we stood on the edge of the pond I could see one small leg sticking out from near the tail. It had to be a calf, cows only have four legs. But only one leg visible? That meant trouble.

Well, I thought to myself, time to venture out on the ice. It's at this stage in your career that you imagine all the worst scenarios possible. The ice will never stand the strain of me, it'll crack and the cow and I will disappear below the surface of the lake, sorry pond, never to be seen again. We could drag her off with a tractor, and in the process the cow, the tractor, the driver, and myself will all disappear below the surface. It wasn't worth thinking about. I'd chance my luck. There's no way the head cow man was coming out there with me, so I reckoned it was a fair chance the ice would support my weight after all, the cow probably outweighed me by about five to one, even with all the Christmas tucker I'd managed to stuff inside.

So far, so good. I knelt down and slid a hand inside. It only took twenty seconds to realise what was going on. Here we had a classic dystocia, in other words, a pretty run-of-the-mill problem birthing situation in cattle: a head and one leg turned back. Let me give you the picture. Most calves are born head first in what we call the diving position. That means both front legs are stretched forward with the head held in between, exactly like someone diving into the water. It makes a nice little wedge that the cow can usually push out without too much difficulty. But in this situation one of the front legs had got caught up with things and instead of pointing forwards it was stretched backwards along the side of the calf, and the head

and neck were turned round as well, as if looking to see where the darn leg had gone. They're not all that difficult to fix, you shove the calf back in a bit, get hold of the nostrils with your fingers, pull the head back into position, then reach alongside the calf, fold the leg up and bring it forward too. Sounds so easy! You probably all think you can do it. But this situation was a little more difficult. For a start the cow was flat out on the ice. And secondly, the only warm place I was to find in the next twenty minutes or so would be the inside of this cow.

Back at the car we did have equipment for situations that were something like this. The practice issued all their vets with a thin oilskin that was supposed to prevent you from getting wet while doing various manipulations lying on the ground. No-one had ever mentioned anything about operating on a skating rink however. As I laid the oilskin out behind the cow, I realised that the only thing between the various parts of my anatomy that really mattered to a young male like myself and the ice over the ensuing minutes would be this flimsy material. The thoughts of the possible end of the Cooper dynasty there on an English pond did prompt me to really get stuck into things. The equipment was laid out on the ice: my khunes crutch to push the calf back; a small set of bulldog clips to grab the calf's nostrils; and a collection of calving ropes and chains to make pulling the very slippery youngster all the easier.

While all this was going on I happened to glance over my shoulder at what from a distance seemed to be some bizarre conga line of dairy workers swaying slowly down the slope toward the pond. Once there, they assembled themselves around the edge of the pond and proceeded to offer less than helpful suggestions as to how I should get on with the job. I have always been able to handle most people and most situations, but post-Christmas revellers are something different. So just what to do with this inebriated mass of manpower was the question. My mind went back to university days and an old professor who had this simple piece of advice: 'In a situation like this always give them something to do.'

Too right I would. Forgetting about the cow and her calf for a minute I went back to the car and rummaged around in the boot for anything that might even resemble a calving rope. Gathering together the most interesting mixture of ropes and chains and other fandangles, I strode back onto the ice, knelt down and got to work. Using a loop, everyone of these ropes was attached to the only leg of the calf that was presented to the outside world. The suggestions were still coming thick and fast, that is until the ropes were laid out along the ice to the very edge. They shut up for a minute and it was time to address the head cow man.

'I want you to make sure these guys pull when I tell them,' I said. Everyone of them held a rope in their hands, and drunk as he was, he demanded their utmost concentration. The language was quite comical. I should tell you that there was no need to be at all articulate when I lived in Wiltshire. All conversations are conducted using just one letter, and it's not even a vowel. 'R' will get you anywhere and everywhere—just as long as you give it the right sort of inflection, all the locals will understand just exactly what is being said!

As I spent the next episode of my life in intimate contact with the layer of ice below and the rear end of this poor cow, I proceeded to call out, 'Pull on one, pull on three.' This kept them all gainfully occupied and, thank heavens, quiet as well. It was of course the one leg that they were all pulling on so finally, after about twenty minutes of pushing and shoving, everything got sorted the way it should be. The head came around and the two legs straightened out nicely. It took another minute or two to swap things around so that now the head and the other leg both had ropes attached. The mob on shore had not the faintest idea of what was going on out there on the ice and under the constant barrage of directions from the head cow man they didn't have a chance to ask either.

It was time to pull again. 'All pull together!' I yelled.

They did. It took no effort at all, just a bit of guidance. Out onto the ice slid a beautiful Friesian heifer, all hot and steamy, like she'd just stepped out of a sauna in her black and white fur coat. It's always a great sight. The head cow man couldn't resist it any longer, and he strode out onto the ice.

Now the very fact that it was a heifer (a female to you who know little about cows) had absolutely nothing to do with me, it was all the bull's fault. But when you're a vet and you've just delivered it, there is a feeling that it does earn bonus points. There I am, lying there huffing and panting on the ice, gathering up my tools of trade, the calf beside me and poor ol' mum trying to get round to look at her new baby. Then this figure stands above me, confident that his efforts alone have resulted in such a splendid outcome. He looks down as I scramble to my feet and in a broad Wiltshire accent enquires, 'What aboot a driink?'

'Gees,' I said, everything about me, excepting my right arm which had spent the best part of the afternoon inside the cow, being numb from the cold, 'I'd love a drink.'

'Not you laddie, bloody calf.'

There never was and there never will be an answer to that. Head bowed, I stumbled back to the car. They were all out there on the ice now. Not one word of thanks. It's often the way.

I slammed the boot closed on the Ford Anglia, turned out of that ancient gate and headed for home. It doesn't matter how and it doesn't matter when, the very act of helping a new living thing to enter our world is thanks enough. This little lady was something special; she was born on Christmas Day. I wonder if animals still know what we seem to have forgotten: the real meaning of Christmas.

9

Parlour Talk

Salisbury was a beautiful city. I guess you could almost call it the capital of Wiltshire. There were two veterinary practices in the town, the other much larger than ours. I shared the workload with the boss and one other vet. They'd had a string of Aussies and Kiwis working with them over the years. I think it's the fact that we tended to work a lot quicker and a lot harder than many of the locals that kept getting us jobs. To me the wonderful thing about England, in particular the country, is that the place is just so English! From the little country pubs, with their darkened, yet warmly welcoming interiors, to the old castles and beautiful cathedrals that were part of the city. There were some ancient ruins from the Roman era as well. It was a great place to live and spend some five months working.

The practice covered a large area around Salisbury, down almost as far as Bournemouth on the coast, up past Stonehenge and through wonderful sounding towns like Bishop's Stortford and Fordingbridge. We spent most of the day in and around the countryside, looking after cattle and, to a lesser degree sheep and horses, usually on our own, although sometimes with a nurse, if we needed a bit of assistance. Communication was by two-way radio. A lot of the work we did was pretty run-of-the-mill, certainly in comparison to what we do back home. The English farmers tended to rely very heavily on the veterinary profession, if anything at all went wrong.

Milk fever is a very common occurrence in high producing cows in progressive dairy herds. It's the common name given to a condition where the blood calcium level drops way below normal and the cow finds herself unable to stand. Changes to her heart rate develop which if untreated can result in the death of the animal. It usually occurs either just before or, more commonly, just after the cow has calved. It's as if she pours all the calcium in her bloodstream into that massive udder, leaving her blood levels far too low.

Treatment is pretty simple. We all carried around bottles of calcium boro gluconate, CBG for short, and a long rubber tube with a needle attached. At the other end was a black rubber device known as a flutter valve which we simply capped over the end of the open bottle, turned it upside down, and the solution ran down through the tube and the attached needle and into the cow. The valve controlled the rate of flow. The needle was inserted in the jugular vein of the cow, in the lower part of the neck, and usually the contents of one bottle were enough to correct the condition in most patients. So my next case should have been pretty simple, but in veterinary practice you learn that it's the simple things that often cause the most problems.

The farm was reasonably close to town, and a really pretty place. Most of the traditional old buildings were constructed of a mixture of flint and bricks. They tended to look very much the same. The corners and door arches, even the window sills, were outlined in the dark, bluey-grey slate typical of the countryside. The stone fragments were small, and held together by an excess of white lime mortar. In between, the brickwork was neat and tidy with the bright, orange-red blocks con-trasting with the darker slate corners. A huge old-fashioned rose clambered over the doorway and tiny wooden porch of this farmhouse. Even in the heart of winter it still had a striking beauty. Though not one leaf remained, the stark wiry branches held the remnants of what no doubt many blackbirds and wrens had called their homes in the warmer months, when its delicious perfume must have filled the whole house.

I'd not been to the place before, but I'd heard that the farmer was a pretty—how shall I say—strict and authoritarian type of individual. He didn't have a cow man, and he didn't have a parlour. Now hang on a minute, you probably wonder what in heaven's name I'm talking about. Well, in Pommie cow talk, a parlour has got nothing to do with a room inside the house. It's quite the opposite. This is outside the house. Here in good old Aussie, we call the same thing our bails or the dairy. Over there, bails were mobile bits of equipment that they towed around a paddock, sorry, field. Poms don't have paddocks. They have meadows, fields, all that sort of stuff. Anyhow, these bails were left over from World War Two, made of wood and roofed with iron, often gaily painted and on wheels. The majority of these contraptions were what we termed 'two, doubled up, walk throughs', which means that you could milk four cows at the one time.

This is probably all very confusing so let me explain a little. Cows are milked twice daily for about nine or ten months of the year. They are often programmed to calve at certain times, usually the spring, to take full advantage of the abundance of fresh grass that's on hand. Pregnancy lasts around nine months, and the calf is weaned off its mum after three or four days and then reared with all the other calves on a milk replacement formula. By the time the cows have calved for the second or third time they are pretty used to the system, and soon settle into the milking routine. Early mornings and mid-afternoons they usually track into the dairy from the pasture to be unburdened of the mass of white, watery goodness we call milk. Today these milking establishments are huge, milking up to one hundred cows at a time on a huge rotary disc that slowly revolves, a far cry from the particular set-up I was about to visit.

As most of the herds in the district were less than a hundred, this fairly archaic sort of set-up probably suited them nicely. They'd leave the bail in the one spot for three or four days and then tow it to another, a hundred metres or so away, and then they'd be ready to go all over again. Nothing to clean up, no need to worry, and all the fertiliser went straight back onto the paddock. Only well-off farmers had parlours. So this guy wasn't all that well off. He was waiting down behind the house, by the side of the gravel driveway at a big old iron gate with huge dry-stone walled gateposts in support. Everything else was hidden behind a high bramble hedge. I parked inside. The lanes were so narrow and the hedges so high, it would have been suicide to leave the car out there. We had quite a walk in front of us.

Some people are natural conversationalists and some are definitely not. He was not. It's hard to talk about nothing at all to someone you've never met before but I was always one to try. This guy however had nothing to say about anything and try as I might to make light of the situation he simply set his jaw, mumbled some sort of curse and lengthened his stride. Strike a light, it was me that was carrying all the wretched gear as well! By the time we tracked across half the damn farm and over several small hills that were beginning to seem like mountains, we finally reached the patient. Sure enough, it was milk fever. Typically twisted neck, felt cold, looked concerned, calved four days ago. All the usual symptoms.

So I hooked her up with the old bottle of CBG, found the jugular vein with ease and inserted the needle. You monitor the heart as you run the calcium in. It's very sensitive to the blood calcium levels and you can tell pretty well how things are going as the heart starts to return to normal. She'd taken the full bottle and things looked to be going fine. Heart sounding normal, pulse good, breathing okay, and that horrible 'S' gone from the neck. It was time for her to get up, something they usually do pretty quickly once things are stabilised. I ran in a bit more calcium under the skin where it would be absorbed slowly over the next few hours, just as an insurance. Still she didn't get up. She looked around, she was bright, she was alert, but she didn't want to get up.

I couldn't see any reason why she wouldn't get to her feet. What was wrong with this damn cow? Sometimes they become injured during calving, but she'd walked out to pasture normally enough so I could rule out calving paralysis. And in this area we didn't encounter any other problems likely to cause this sort of situation. I reckoned she was just stubborn!

Now every vet I've ever met has got some trick or another for getting lazy cows on their feet. Well, I walked around and around this cow for ten minutes pointing at this and that in the distance to distract the farmer's attention, whilst I tried some trick or other on that rotten cow. Nothing seemed to be working. All this time my farmer friend said absolutely nothing, just kept muttering things under his breath that were totally unintelligible, while he too walked round and round the beast looking alternately up to the heavens and into the distance. It was time for the one method that never seems to fail. I grabbed the cow's tail and twisted it round towards her head and gave a push. Yes, it does hurt. It's meant to. It sort of jolts them back to reality. And sure enough she let out an agonised moo and sprang to her feet. I'm sure if she'd been on stage, she'd have been harassed for over-acting. It really doesn't hurt that much. The old girl seemed relieved that at last she was able to stand again and promptly lowered her head to the ground, grabbed a little of what grass remained after the recent snows, and slowly wandered off to join the rest of the herd.

But I could sense straightaway that this straightlaced farming client of mine wasn't too happy. Yet it was my job and my belief that I should never leave the scene of a milk fever until the cow was on her feet. And let's face it, I didn't have all day. By the time I got back to the office that night he'd been on to the boss and given him a right ol' serve about this Aussie bloke who might know what he's doing but is a bit rough on the stock. There was no lecture. Like I said, lots of Aussies had worked in this practice and I think we were all cast in very much the same mould. But I was asked to be just a little more careful next time.

You wouldn't believe it, no more than forty-eight hours later, I'm back at the same farm, with the same bloke with the same problem, but with a different cow. The case was an absolute deadringer of the first one. An obvious milk fever in a huge Friesian with a massive udder, his top producing cow. In goes the CBG, heart sounds normal, nothing else wrong, won't get up.

◆

Those of you who know me today probably don't realise that in the early part of my life I used to wear a hat. In the land of Oz it was an Akubra. Very much the Slim Dusty type with the brim turned down at the front and a fairly plain band around the head. Usually a fawny colour and somehow it always took two or three lengths of the pool underwater with the hat on to get it bashed into the shape I liked. It just didn't seem right to wear one of these in Pommie Land. So I'd bought myself a little tweed number. It was very much like the caps I wear today. Made from patches and pieces of different material sewn together in a little round thing with a nice narrow brim. You needed something to keep your head warm in a Wiltshire winter, when the days could be frozen from dawn to dusk. There were times when I drove for nine days on end without turning off my headlights. As a matter of fact, I used to smoke a pipe as well and wrap my hands around the bowl to keep them warm. The heater in the old Ford Anglia was cactus!

When you're working with cows you tend to spend about half your time at the rear end. As a matter of fact, when I first decided on veterinary science as a career, the adviser who interviewed me at the time intimated that in this particular profession you would spend half your life with your hand or your finger up one end or down the other. Cripes he was right. Well, a little tweed cap with a little narrow brim can get a little soiled when you've got your right arm buried up to the shoulder. So I'd made a habit of taking it off and folding it. It was pretty malleable and I'd simply flatten the whole thing to form a sort of triangle with the brim at the base and then fold it again still with the brim at the base to make it half as wide and very narrow and pointed. That way I could shove it in my hip pocket.

I walked around and around this wretched cow, cursing and swearing, under my breath of course, and calling it every sort of mongrel under the sun for not getting up. I tried all the tricks. Nothing worked. In desperation, I walked to the front of the cow, looked it square in the eye, took the hat out of my back pocket, went to put it on my head, but instead flicked it backwards and forwards over the cow's face. 'Get up you damn stupid thing,' I said. And by God it did.

'Aye,' said the farmer, 'the maan wid d comigal at.'

By the time I got to town every damn person in the joint seemed to know I was the man with the comical hat. Still, it was good for a free beer occasionally. And don't let them tell you that Pommie beer's no good. All beers are good; it's just that some are better than others.

10

Just Like Old Times

A lot can happen in twenty years. Some people say it's wrong to go back; you should never revisit places that you treasure in your memory. Somehow they never seem quite the same. I reckon that's true, for some things in life. To go back to homes that we've owned has always been an anti-climax. While the garden and all the landscaping were my domain, the house, the furnishings and the inside were Janine's. Plants and flowers once loved and treasured are left to languish, whilst colour schemes and wallpapers planned with such loving thought are changed overnight to some unfamiliar and in some ways dis-cordant tones. I guess other people's interests are different to our own and their outlook on life and their priorities at odds with what we like and plan. But it's not always true. There have been things and places that I've gone back to and they have been every bit as good as the day I left them. This is a story about one of those dearly cherished places from the past.

It was some three years into 'Talk to the Animals', and we were filming for one of our special episodes in England and Ireland. We'd been all over the place from Devon and Cornwall in the south-west, up the west coast to Bath and Bristol then on up to Inverness and Loch Ness in the lower half of Scotland. Travelling all around the beautiful west coast of Ireland around Galway and Killarney and finally back to London was just a truly wonderful experience. And Janine had enjoyed it too.

After all it was her first trip to 'the mother country'.

It was quite a large undertaking to transport two camera crews with all their gear, a field producer and some five reporters all that way, and have everything go exactly as planned. Even the notorious British weather was on our side and very few days were lost due to rain. There were of course different animals to see and different people to meet, and even though I'd worked in the United Kingdom as a young vet not all that long out of university, lots had changed. It was different to the normal filming back home, as these stories were far longer and more detailed, destined to be part of an extended episode, which proved a real winner when it finally went to air.

The publicity department at the Seven Network knew that I'd worked in Salisbury in the south-west of England and thought it'd be a good idea to revisit the past and see if I could meet up with some of the people in a few of the places where I'd lived and worked for nearly six months. A photographer and I set out early one Sunday morning from London and as we drove down the well-known road all the names of those little places came flooding back. Down the M3, gee, it used to be the A30 and the A33 when I was there. So we pulled off at Basingstoke and took the old road, which became the 303, we'd bypassed Andover and then down through Stockbridge, past Middle Wallop, Over Wallop and on towards our goal. Middle Winterslow, West Grimstead, Coombe Bissett—it had been twenty years, well perhaps a few more, and in spite of the wretched ring road, I still knew where to go. These ring roads seem to be something of a trend as we rocket into the twenty-first century. Every decent-sized town and city in

England has to have one. You just haven't made it if the bitumen hasn't totally encircled the place like a hangman's noose threatening to choke the very life out of the joint. The obvious tall landmarks still remained and almost as though I'd never really been away for more than a month or two the car took the off ramp and we drove into the city of Salisbury.

The parking area was where it had always been, right in the middle of town. It used to be free, but not any more. Salisbury is a very popular tourist destination these days, so having done our little bit to support the local council and the parking officers by paying, it was time to look around.

Right next door was the Poultry Cross, a wonderful old stone God-knows-what standing slap bang in the middle of the one-way system. It was a peculiar building, not all that big, but with several archways and a domed roof. I never did find out what it was for, but I think it had something to do with the place being an early market town. First stop was the bookshop. I'd spent many hours and quite a few quid in this little shop, and it was only a few minutes walking distance on the way to the magnificent cathedral. The shop stood on a corner. It was a beautiful old building with heavy timber windows, glazed with that funny old-fashioned stuff that looks like reject materials from the bottom of wine bottles—you know that circular sort of material that you can't see through, but looks good anyhow. Inside it was musty and a little damp. The proprietor used to wear these funny sort of half glasses. Just the bottom bit. He could see pretty well over the top. He'd gone now, and yet I could still see him, even feel his presence. He had worn an almost perpetual smile that had drawn his warm, reddened face into a series of deep horizontal lines. There was little hair to grace his temples and the tweed waistcoat that buttoned tightly around his middle always looked a couple of sizes too small. Those buttons must have been made of pretty tough stuff.

His son had taken over, and the shop had fallen on hard times. In the window was a message which I copied down: 'The proprietors and staff would like to thank their valued customers for their patronage over the preceding years. Declining volume of sales and increased expenditure will force the doors of this store to close on August 30, 1996.' That was next Friday. Fate had delivered me here just before another of life's past treasured memories had been wiped from the earth. I was one of those valued customers, and I was here. I felt good about that, nice and warm inside, but sad too. We took some stills inside and outside the shop. Did the young owner remember me? Sadly no. After all he was only about twelve at the time and I was only one of many who must have passed through those doors over the years.

Sometimes you need something tangible to hang onto. A material object that can be looked back upon to help the brain recall a particular event. Haven't you ever felt like that? There are so many thing that lie around our home, often just little things, but all are treasured for every one can conjure up some shared experience, some happy memory, a little piece of our own history to have forever.

I bought a book. I had to. If time had allowed there would have been more. *A Guide to Salisbury*. He signed inside the cover, and both he and I shared the same feeling of sadness about the passing of what had to be one of Salisbury's institutions. So much for our wonderful world of technical achievements. When our bookshops start closing, our civilisation is going backwards, not forwards. How many civilisations in the past have lost their books and lost their way? I believe we must always make the time to read, and teach our children and their children the same habit.

The cathedral stood close by. It had been our local church and was still being restored twenty years down the track. The scaffolding's still there. How is it every time you want to visit a historic building in Europe, the damn thing is in hairpins? Happens all the time. It's gotta be a conspiracy. The cathedral is a stunning building with a spire that dominates the surrounding countryside. It's a huge piece of architecture by any standard, set centrally amidst a sweeping green lawn. Going inside, nothing had changed. There were sightseers everywhere; the reverence of the building seemed almost to have been lost. Visitors seemed more intent on photographing this and that rather than just sitting quietly and letting the ambience of the place fill you. I knelt for a few minutes in one of the back pews and remembered Christmas Day here all those years ago. What a disappointment. Such a magnificent building, there had been fewer people in the congregation than there were in the choir stalls. Twelve of us, twenty-two of them. And in one of the most inspiring buildings ever constructed.

Time was marching on by now and the worms were starting to bite about halfway down our intestinal tracts. Lunch seemed like a good idea. It was time to visit the old watering hole. There is nothing in the world even remotely like an English pub. The Haunch of Venison was built around 1460. That makes it pretty old. I used to spend many a night with friends inside that wonderful old pub. It was tiny. Really tiny. The front room only had space for two men and a dog. And fair dinkum, that's usually exactly what you found there. Off to the left on the other side of the door was the parlour. This was more spacious, with room for upwards of twenty people. There was usually a large fire burning at the far end and it was customary on Sunday nights to roast chestnuts under the fire grate.

The first time I walked in was one Sunday night. My then wife plonked down on one of the old church pews that lined the wall of the parlour and I popped over to the bar for a couple of drinks. The bar area was all polished brass and old timber, with the sort of ambience that's impossible to properly describe. The beer comes up from the cellar by pump. Using a large ceramic handle with a huge brass engine under the bar, the barman delivers the amber fluid to the huge glasses under the taps. People only drink beer in pints and half pints. It's as flat as rain-water, and a bit the same sort of temperature as well. But you get used to it, and even get to like it. It took a good few minutes to grab the drinks. After all, just what sort of beer do you order when you are in such a strange land and the beer that they sell in Wiltshire is very different to the beer that they sold up closer to London. So of course a man needs the advice of the publican as to just what is the best on tap.

By the time I turned around, there was no sign of my wife. Instead, there was a congregation of every possible English character from any Dickensian novel you would wish to meet. There was the gamekeeper with his shotgun propped in the corner, muddy boots and muddy trousers, flannelette shirt and tweed coat, with a hat, wet and soggy, pulled down over one ear. The business executive in his pinstripe suit, complete with the red carnation, the dark tie, the white shirt and the black bowler hat, umbrella and briefcase still tucked under the arm. A tall, thin, tanned individual with a pencil-thin moustache carefully twirled and worked till it extended some inches on both sides of his mouth. He'd flown Hurricanes in the Battle of Britain. Even the law was represented. The local constable, still in uniform, but with the familiar helmet parked somewhere out of sight. Not everyone looked to be above the law either. There was this shady looking character. I reckon he had to be a poacher. Two or three days' growth of stubble covered his thin, shrivelled face and his hands were gnarled and twisted as an ancient tree. And there, like some star attraction for the night, in the middle of the lot of them was my wife. Sure there were other ladies there too, and many other characters of the district, most of whom were to become our good friends over the next few months. We became regulars and threw in each weekend for the chestnut roast, where the warm offerings were passed around on a fire tool along with a plate loaded with salt in which to dunk the roasted nuts.

Upstairs were two other bars and a dining room. None of the walls were perpendicular. All the floors sloped in one direction or another. Even the ceilings had an unnatural belly right in the centre. And there was a spot halfway up a narrow flight of stairs where a man's hand had been neatly encased in the ancient lime mortar between some ageing brickwork, right alongside a secret passage which was said to have hidden the local bishop during one of the purges of the local clerics. All of this, right there in my 'regular'.

We had lunch and rummaged through some leaflets on the pub's history. So much had happened within these walls. They must have been sordid days. The pub had changed hands, several times, since I'd left. But the atmosphere hadn't. No gaming machines here. No rattle and bang, no loud music, just relaxation, good tucker, and the same flat beer. Even after all this time it still tasted okay. You never really do forget.

◆

We drove to the old building that used to house the veterinary practice where I was employed. It was just a short way out of town on the road down the Woodford Valley, up on the right it stood, a double-storey stone building, grey and cold as always, with a circular driveway out the front and a parking area at the rear. They'd sealed the car park with black asphalt and now it looked even colder than usual. You wouldn't believe it, standing right at the front entrance, fiddling around with something in the boot of his car, was Graham. He and I had been the assistants to the senior partner, Jim Bruford, all those years ago. Jim had died some ten years after I left, and now Graham ran the practice, with the help of a young female veterinarian. Graham was a tall thin fella with a long shock of wavy hair, still as long as ever, and still overdue for a haircut that somehow he never found time for. We talked about old times and had a look through the establishment. A little bit of paint here and there, a new kennel block and operating theatre; not much else had changed.

For the locum in the practice they were obliged to provide accommodation, so we used to live upstairs, above the practice itself. It was freezing. Damn freezing! Every room had its own gas fire and it was a bit of a competition to get up each morning and see if you could light every fire with just one match. We soon gave up on this; better to keep the damn things burning all night. Work kept me here from December right through till May, without a doubt the coldest, most miserable time of the year, and doubly so on the windswept Salisbury plain. We'd hired a fridge and no-one could understand why. But it was the go for the milk and the beer. There was a spare room at the back of the upstairs. I think it once housed the toilet. It had a dirty great big hole in the floor and was suspended out in mid-air. The wind would rush up through this hole and the room was constantly at a temperature only fractionally above freezing. We kept all our vegies in there, and the door very tightly closed.

I'd done as every other Aussie before me had most likely done. With only three days left on my contract in Salisbury, I'd managed to prang the Anglia. Just as James Herriot drove around in a little old car making house calls to all his beloved clients in the Yorkshire Dales, so I was given a Ford Anglia. They were small, four-cylinder jobs that could get along a bit, but handled like a melting blancmange. The boot and most of the back seat were full of veterinary equipment, and because we were dealing with large animals, most of the equipment was pretty substantial and awkward to carry around. We had two-way radios installed to keep us up to date on any emergency that may need our urgent attention while we negotiated the narrow country lanes and hedge-lined byways that made working here just so different to home. Everyone and everything seemed to have or take so much more time. The weather aside, it was a pleasant lifestyle.

The Anglia was the smallest car in the entire practice. Everyone else drove six-cylinder Ford Zephyrs. One day I was meandering down a side road on the way to the local military base, Bulford Camp, sliding around the familiar corner, in a perfectly controlled four-wheel drift, when, oops-a-daisy. The council had been at it and the road was covered in a slippery muddy clay. The four-wheel drift wasn't all that controlled anymore, and to make matters worse, suddenly this other bloke was coming straight for me. The road was normally wide enough for two, but unfortunately I was going sideways and I was in the middle. He was very pleasant about the whole thing. The damage was only slight to his Morris Minor, but a bit more substantial to the old Anglia.

The local constabulary duly arrived and were very pleasant about things. I explained that everything would have been just fine had the other car not been in the way, and I'm sure he understood my point of view. It seemed like it at the time anyway. Sure enough, the ticket arrived. Don't they always? 'Driving without due care and attention. Penalty: five pounds.' No points in those days! The spare Zephyr was mine for the last three days.

Leaving the practice in Salisbury was sad. It was time to go back to Cheshunt, our base near London, and do some small animals work for a week or two before the next country assignment. The last night saw a great farewell party down at the Wheat Sheaf at Lower Woodford, just down the road from the practice. No breathalysers in those days and it was only a ten-minute run straight up the valley road. With the river on one side and huge open meadows on the other, you couldn't get lost. The publican here had become quite friendly and one sunny Sunday afternoon had sought my earnest opinion—'being an Australian and of course a drinker of lager-style beers'—on a beer he was about to install. There were—and hopefully still are—many small, boutique breweries right around England. Each area has its own special ales or beers. Most are flat as mentioned before but what he sought to install was a beer like ours, propelled by gas and so with a head, that came up from the barrel under pressure. Not only that, it was served cold!

I forget the name of the maker but the trade name was 'Badger'. He poured me a sample glass. It was seventy per cent froth and very little beer. It tasted putrid.

'Strike,' I said. 'There must be something dead in the tank.' Possibly one of their badgers, I thought. The stuff did improve with time. Or maybe my tastebuds wilted under pressure. But once the whole delivery system bedded in, the brew became quite popular with the locals. We all consumed quite a drop that night.

Departure day finally came and it was time to settle the accounts. All our worldly goods were piled into the back of a little red Mini station sedan, complete with the woodwork around the back. They were called 'Estates' if I'm not mistaken. In the front the two of us and a dog, a greyhound called Ginger. She would go on to win thirty-two races for us in London, but you'll read about her later on. She was special.

The practice accountant called out. He wanted a word before we left. Blowed if I can remember his name, but he was a short, overweight, ageing man, always dressed in a suit and tie, the knot of which was always so badly tied that the broad end of the garment always finished some six inches shorter than the thin end. He huffed and puffed his way around the building on a once-a-week basis for a couple of hours, trying to keep the practice financial records in some sort of order.

'It's about this gas bill.'

'What about the gas bill?' I asked. 'It's the employer's responsibility.'

'Yes, but it's nearly three hundred pounds.'

'That's ridiculous,' I said. 'The meter has got to be out, or there's got to be a leak, or it must be for the practice too.'

'You're right,' he said, 'of course, there's a mistake. I mean, to get that sort of gas bill, you'd've had to have had all the heaters burning day and night.' Little did he know.

◆

It was time for us to push on. There were still other memories to relive. Still time though for a nostalgic drive down the Woodford Valley past pubs that I knew so well with their thatched roofs and black-painted Tudor exteriors, advertising beers that only the locals would know, full of patrons soaking up the brilliant autumn sunshine and basking in the last of warmth left over from summer. Past familiar farm gates, each one with its own memories of cases seen and farmers met, of huge afternoon teas and scones piled high with home-made strawberry jam and clotted cream, of nights spent drinking mangol wine concocted from huge turnips, and of hearty hand-shakes from huge palms, deeply furrowed like the fields that they ploughed. The farming community really valued their vets in those days.

Then back through the centre of town on the very last part of my journey of recollection. I was looking here for a farm. A special farm, a farm where they grow watercress. Have you ever seen the stuff? It grows wild down here in Tassie where we live these days (and we live here because it reminds us very much of rural England). You can often find it along the edges of quietly flowing little country streams, for it needs to live in water. Harvesting the stuff is easy. Just cut off the last six or eight inches, and there you have it. With hard-boiled egg sand-wiches or in salads with a good egg mayonnaise you can't beat the stuff. It's a little hot, but it's full of flavour.

As we wended our way slowly up the Chalke Valley, past Bishopstone, Stoke Farthing, Broad Chalke and Bower Chalke, I searched in vain for a familiar landmark. But my memory let me down. It had to be around somewhere but just where I couldn't remember. At last a farmer came walking slowly towards us, right down the middle of the road as if he owned the place, with a dozen or so black-faced sheep in front. His border collie was weaving backwards and forwards behind the group, her eyes never leaving the woolly animals in her charge. It was getting late in the day and he seemed a little hard of hearing. Out of the car I jumped.

'Do you know any watercress places around here?' I asked.

'You'd be a stranger here then,' he says.

'Yeah,' I said. 'Used to work around here some twenty years ago, for Dalton and Bruford, the vets in town.'

'That's a long time, lad,' he said. (Fancy calling me a lad! I'm over fifty, but then I suppose he was well over seventy.) 'Jim's been dead a fair time and Dalton, well heaven knows what happened to him, most of the farms have gone, closed up, pulled down, only one left.'

'Where's that?' I asked.

'Well lad,' he continued, 'turn back around, go one mile, take right fork, over bridge, go bit further, through big gate, that be it.'

Only one left, of all the little farmhouses with their three or four weirs spanning the creek from shore to shore. Each bed some two or so feet deep and full of lush green cress. The water flowed slowly in the top end and out the bottom, the whole thing controlled by a series of sluice gates. The water wash was just right. Flowing over chalky country for thousands of years it was pure and clear, ideal for the crop that flourished right in its midst. This was what the chalk valley was all about. What, I wondered, did these people do today? Was this yet another sacrifice to progress? Only one left. Would it be the one?

Away we went, following the river up the familiar valley. Turned as the old farmer had said and suddenly it was like someone had switched on the light. I knew where I was, this was the place, the very place, where I'd come every Friday afternoon to buy my two bunches of cress, enough to last for the whole week. There didn't look to be too much of the stuff around though. All but one of the huge ponds was empty, no doubt waiting to be replanted. Otherwise nothing had changed here. Just as it had always been and was twenty-odd years ago. At the back of the parking area was a shed. The same shed, unpainted corrugated iron, more like something you'd see back in Australia than in the Wiltshire countryside. Still with the same gloomy interior, same huge sliding door, still open a foot or two as it always was. I got out. I just wanted to do this myself. I walked slowly towards the shed and in through the door. It was dark inside, very, very dark. But somehow I felt that there was someone there too. And in the faint light in the back corner I could see a figure, hunched over, working, just as I'd seen a similar figure twenty years ago. I think his back was permanently bowed from stooping to pick up the cress and bind it into bunches for the market.

It was too much to hope. Would the last piece of the jigsaw fall into place? Would or could this shadowy figure in the corner be the same bloke I used to buy from all those years ago? Too much to ask? It was worth a go.

'Any chance of a bunch of cress?'

He never even looked up. He never even moved. But he did speak.

'Aye, lad, the maan wid d comigal at.'

God, I started to cry. I couldn't believe it. I went over and hugged him. He must have thought I was a bloody idiot. I didn't care. 'How, after twenty years, could you possibly remember me?'

'Well lad,' he said, 'how many people come in here and ask for a bunch of cress with an Australian accent?'

He wouldn't accept one penny for the cress, nothing at all. We talked for a while about old times and how the valley was changing. He would live out his life here but the future was something he cared not to think about. There was time for photos in that lovely orange light of an English autumn afternoon. It's so soft and golden, peaceful and yet warm. There will always be an England, and for me on this day there could not have been a better place anywhere in the world. After all this time I'd come back, and found enough of what I left behind to make it all worthwhile. And certainly enough to make me want to come back again one day.

Kennels and Tracks

11

The Hull Story

The city of Hull lies on the east coast of England at the mouth of the Humber River. It's near Leeds and York and not too far away from James Herriot country. As a young vet working in England you got jobs in many different places and Hull was one of those. To tell the truth I wasn't all that keen on going. The place had somewhat of a reputation as a heavily industrial, dirty sort of city, but this was definitely not the case. It was an interesting place, really badly bombed during World War Two and at least half of it must have been flattened. On recollection, it's a shame they didn't flatten the lot and start all over again. Many of the buildings looked like typical Australian corrugated, half-cylindrical, long huts, the sort of things that were used after the war to house so many of our new immigrants. I guess they were a sort of temporary accommodation for people who had lost their homes in the German onslaught. It was just a shame that even all this time later they hadn't been replaced. Other areas of the city were modern mixtures of glass, steel and concrete, the sort of thing that makes most cities around the world look disappointingly the same. But there were quaint parts of the city too, parts that had avoided damage and had character and history all of their own.

Large hovercraft crisscrossed the river at regular intervals and their shower of spray would make a spectacular sight, especially when the wind roared in off the sea. There was in fact a lot to recommend the place.

The practice in which I was employed back then was owned and run single-handedly by an ageing vet who, interestingly enough, was heavily involved in alternative medicine. He had cupboard after cupboard stocked full of some of the most bizarre herbal and homoeopathic concoctions I've ever come across. Having an open mind on this subject is an advantage and I spent a lot of my time in the practice rummaging through his collection of books on the subject trying to gain some sort of insight into what he was about. All of this may have been some thirty years ago, and now it seems that both veterinary and human medicine are realising that there is in fact quite a deal of worth in so many of these treatments. I have little doubt that in years to come we will find more and more use for these traditional medicines.

The set-up of the practice was the most incredible thing I'd ever seen. It was a long, narrow two-storey house, built right up to the footpath. Yep, there was no front garden, just the pavement. In the front of the house, to the right, was a single-car garage, with a large tilting door. Alongside it was the front door and a corridor that ran the full length of the house ending in the kitchen towards the rear. On the other side of the corridor, opposite the garage, were the study, the dining room, and the lounge room. Bedrooms and toilets were all upstairs. His consulting room was a small shed, stuck on—and I mean stuck on—to the rear of the house. All the drugs, dressings and bandages were stored along the walls of the corridor. Surgery hours were from nine to eleven in the morning and five to seven at night. The family ate at six o'clock. How they managed to maintain any sort of dignity was totally beyond me.

When it came time for surgery this distinguished veterinary gentleman simply opened the garage door, backed out the car, set up two or three folding chairs, and pulled down the door again. The clients came in via his own front door and made a right-hand turn into the waiting room, which was of course the garage. Get the picture? The floor was covered with by now badly damaged black lino tiles. Oil had leaked from his vehicle over the years and tended to play havoc with the glue holding the tiles to the floor. It was pretty austere I can tell you! And cold as well! His reception area was a small desk stuck in the middle of the corridor. There was a phone directly over the top and his poor wife, or whichever family member happened to be on duty that particular night, served as his receptionist. It was a pretty tight squeeze past all of this, because you walked into the garage, picked up your client—metaphorically speaking of course—and carted them right down the centre of the house, past the study, past the lounge room, past the dining room, through the kitchen and out the back door. I don't know how he ever did it. We managed. The people were a humble lot and just seemed to take the whole thing as a matter of course, with a 'hello' or 'good morning' as the case may be when they passed any of the family enjoying a meal in the dining room.

He worked seven days a week. I didn't work Sundays, and told him that. Besides, most Aussie vets could get through half as much again in a day as the locals. When I took the job it was on the understanding that it was basically small animal—and that means just dogs and cats really, with the odd bird, rabbit, guinea pig and these funny little guys called hamsters as well. Quite honestly hamsters didn't like me much and the feeling was mutual. They could turn themselves inside out in their own skin and bite in rapid-fire succession, almost without provocation. We don't have them in Australia, a situation I am entirely grateful for.

Sure, I could handle the horse work too, but he assured me when I arrived that there were only a dozen or so horse clients. Oh yeah, and three or four piggeries too. But they wouldn't be a problem. He'd no sooner left the premises than twenty-two pigs dropped dead that night! I've got to be honest folks, I didn't know a lot about pigs, but I was about to embark on a pretty steep learning curve. These piggeries were no small-scale set-ups. Each had over a hundred breeding sows and one could produce an average of eight to ten piglets per litter. Add that up if you can and we had a disaster with a capital 'D'. Autopsy followed autopsy, samples were collected and sent to the government lab, inspectors came and went, the pigs kept dying. But hats off to the British government vets for their attention to detail. It was only three days later that we had effective treatment and prevention to hand and the whole disaster came to an abrupt end. They really knew their stuff, and I came away knowing a lot more about pigs than when I first started. But I've still made a point of avoiding them ever since.

House calls around the city were intriguing, particularly if you had an address in the old area of town. It could go something like this: Mrs Thomas, 7 Gilbert Close, Farm Lane, Harris Court, High Street, followed by one of the suburbs. You learnt that you could only take your vehicle so far. Even if it was a little Mini Estate. In fact, High Street is probably as far as you could go. You then got out, grabbed the old black bag, locked up and headed off. Harris Court was a narrow lane between two tall buildings. With a bit of pushing and shoving you may just have got a very small car down its length. It opened onto several laneways. These were little more than pedestrian alleys, although I suppose in days gone by, people could have pushed carts up and down them. And again off these lanes ran little dead-end closes, with about a dozen or so tenement style houses clustered around them. Some were pretty, with colourful gardens full of red geraniums, or bright yellow marigolds in stark contrast to the dull grey walls of the houses behind. Many had window boxes or windowsills full of ornamental plants. You really did need something to brighten up the landscape.

The people themselves were happy people. They loved their animals to the point where sometimes I think love tended to overrule any semblance of commonsense. They kept cats and small dogs. Cavaliers, poodles, Maltese and toy terriers were the favourites, along with a motley collection of very scrawny cats and equally unappealing crossbred dogs. While most owners could manage their animals with little or no problem, there was of course the exception. Isn't there always?

Often the culprit was a Jack Russell terrier, and the owner an ageing spinster, at least an octogenarian. Clara really liked me. She must have. She had me making a visit every three or four days to her little tenement. It always had to be the afternoon, that way little Petie would be sure to be exhibiting the wheezing symptoms she could so ably mimic over the telephone. Besides there was the compulsory afternoon tea! It must have been a lonely life for the two of them, and looking back now I do hope my visits did a little to brighten up their day.

After the first visit I was a little better prepared, but initially it was total shock and round one went to the dog. The house was a pretty one, Clara was a keen gardener, and the place looked truly gorgeous. The little wooden gate swung open, I smelled the roses along the pathway to the front door, reached up and rapped the knocker two or three times. World War Three erupted behind that simple wooden door. The sound of a Jack Russell going off his tree, echoing up and down the corridor of an ancient dwelling, starts to sound like a cavalry charge from the front door. She was such a lovely, sweet little old lady, standing there with the dog by her side looking at me as if I were Jack the Ripper about to bring his mistress's life abruptly to an end.

'Do come in,' she said.

I did.

'Where can we go so I can have a good look at him?' I asked.

'Oh, you haven't met Petie before, have you?'

'No,' I explained. 'I'm the locum vet, just filling in.'

She put Petie up on the dining room table and beckoned me over. 'Petie,' she said, 'say hello to the nice young vet.'

Slowly I advanced a hand in the dog's general direction. Petie however was quicker than me. He missed my hand, but tore off a fair chunk of my sleeve. Ah well, you can always buy another shirt, but it's hard to get replacement hands.

So how do you handle a six-kilo bundle of dynamite, intent on having me for afternoon tea?

'Petie really does like you,' Clara continued. 'He's always a bit nervous around strangers.'

He was nervous? How do you think I felt! There was no physical way Clara was going to be able to hold this little bloke, so it was all going to be up to me. Time for a break. What about some history? I needed to know what the problem was, how long it had been going on, and what sort of treatment Petie had been taking.

My little canine aggressor was about nine years old, and had been wheezing and coughing when excited for the last three months. Petie was a problem too; he wouldn't take any of his medication. This meant I had to listen to this little bloke's chest. Believe you me, it wasn't going to be easy.

On many occasions a consultation of this kind simply involved examining the animal from a distance. Many of the residents were fairly elderly, and the dogs knew it, and took complete control. I can see it now. A feisty little Jack Russell charging round and round the living room with this dear old soul standing in the middle, calmly calling, 'Come on Petie, come on Petie, the doctor's here to see you.'

Petie was intent on getting as far away from that damn doctor as he possibly could. And he would soon show his complete objection to the whole procedure by baring his teeth, salivating heavily, rolling back his lips whilst growling and barking in a most threatening manner. It did at least give me a chance to look at his teeth and the colour of his mucous membranes.

As time went by things hotted up. My client would struggle out of her old lounge chair, walking stick in hand and struggle across the floor, almost tripping over the tattered woollen rug which covered most of the area in between the mismatched lounges. 'Come on Petie, come on Petie,' she would say, waving her stick. 'The doctor's not going to hurt you.'

This signal from his owner seemed to turn Petie from defence mode into full-blown attack. He would charge out from behind the large three-seater lounge, dart at your ankles and then rush for cover again, either behind his mother, or the lounge. Examination under these circumstances was difficult, to say the least. Attempts at grabbing the dog were usually met with another ferocious onslaught. Thank God, he only weighed about six kilos. But it was six kilos of fighting tenacity. Jack Russells are normally great little dogs. But over in the United Kingdom their legs are a bit longer and their temper a bit shorter. Most of the examination was done with me kneeling on the lounge and looking over the back at this aggressive canine bundle. I had no chance of getting a lead on him. And if ever I did, he'd spend the whole time trying to do a bunk, ripping and tugging to the accompaniment of the usual excretion of both solid and fluid effluent from his rear end.

Dosing the dog became somewhat of a chore as well. Quite frankly I couldn't imagine any of these devoted yet ageing owners opening their dogs' mouths and shoving a tablet down. If I couldn't get an injection in to start the ball rolling we were in big trouble. The lounge provided cover for the dog, protection for me and one arm of a trap I learnt to spring. About quarter of an hour into the consultation the dog and I had sussed one another out. Only trouble was he knew the layout of the lounge room much better than me, because that was where he lived. It's hard to fool dogs; they're quicker than we are. And it didn't seem to help that I'd been down this path before.

Experience is useless if you don't profit from it. So I decided to spring my lounge room trap. It was just a matter of manipulating the lounge into the corner of the room, leaving just enough opening at one end for the dog to run behind. Once you got him in there the battle was over. Trapped behind the lounge all he could do was jump and bark at me as I leered over the top. Step two. Bombard the dog with cushions. I would gather all the cushions from all the chairs in the room and throw them holus-bolus over the back of the lounge. Then a quick vault over the back. Gotcha! And this defiant little dog meets his match.

Now you had to have everything just right. Syringe in hand, or in back pocket, and once pinned under a pile of cushions, you could slip in the dreaded hypodermic by carefully manipulating a leg from underneath the pile of kapok and velvet. Boy, what an experience! And all the time, in the background, I could hear, 'There's a good boy, Petie. Be a good boy for the doctor.'

On my first weekend the son of my boss came home. He was an architect, a pretty bright lad about my age. We got talking and discovered we had lots of things in common, both of us being not all that long out of university. He had an interest in all sorts of wildlife and in particular the management of the reserves on the Yorkshire Moors. There was quite a large population of New Forest ponies running on a reserve not all that far away from where we were. The problem with so many of these wild horse herds is that they tend to overbreed, the numbers increasing to such a degree that they literally run out of food. The answer then is to desex as many of the males as possible, leaving just one or two stallions for the whole area. It helped to prevent fighting as well.

'Why don't we duck out and do a few?' I suggested. 'Your dad's got all the gear and the drugs.'

'Oh cripes,' he said. 'Dad only does one at a time.'

'Go on, you've got to be joking. Nobody rides them do they?'

'No, they're only wild ponies.'

'Well I reckon we could do a heap in an afternoon.'

I don't really think he believed me. Still, the ranger and some of the local lads managed to get quite a large mob into one of the yards on the edge of the moorland, which were built especially for working with the local cattle. Come Sunday morning we were on our way. Boy oh boy, were they a wild lot—totally unhandled, and pretty terrified of the whole situation. Over time, we managed to draft off most of the colts and stallions. There were about eight or nine big ones, probably two or three smaller ones as well. This was going to be a real cowboy affair and I was beginning to have second thoughts about the whole procedure. Still, it'd been me who'd suggested it, so I thought we had better get on with things.

Being cattle yards, there was a race—a long narrow type of yard into which we were able to run our patients and at least get a rope around their necks. Holding them still was half the battle, but we soon got the timing off pat. I would slip the anaesthetic into their jugular vein and we had about twenty seconds to get them out of the race before they hit the ground. When we got into full swing we were doing one every ten or twelve minutes and by the end we'd done at least a dozen. Not one mishap, not one problem. Over the next week or so our little exploit seemed to take on something of a legendary status. That's all anybody wanted to talk about around the place. I guess it's just the difference between the way we do things and the way they did things.

Sundays were special days. They gave me a chance to explore parts of England that I'd only ever read about. I had a habit of getting up at my usual hour to enjoy a typical English breakfast of bacon, black pudding, egg and fried bread. The housekeeper was a great cook and I didn't have time for this during the week. Then I'd grab a copy of a local paper and head out into the countryside. I'd be in no hurry and often I'd strike one of those beautiful English summer days which, when they come along, really are magnificent. After all the cold and misery of a northern hemisphere winter, the sun really does feel great. I mightn't have quite known where I was headed, but you can never really get lost in England, the roads are just so well signposted and numbered. Nevertheless things don't get interesting until you get onto at least a B or C class road. Don't really know where the pub was either, but it looked inviting and it was after twelve, and hang it all I was hungry.

Nobody makes a ploughman's lunch like an English pub. Two or three thick slices of crusty, doughy bread, a chunk of cheese—and not a miserable slice or wedge, but a dirty great big chunk—a dobble of pickles, a big pickled onion and that's it. None of your fancy lettuce, and all the other carry-on. On the bar there'd be a large glass jar, filled with what at first I took for pickled onions. Wrong. They were pickled eggs. Hard-boiled eggs that had been shelled and then pickled in brown vinegar and boy were they good. I always grabbed one or two of those as well. A pint of the local bitter in a large glass mug or, if I could talk the publican into it, a pewter tankard and I was right. Sitting in the garden, woolfing into my tucker, everything was right with the world.

A warm afternoon, a full stomach and a pint of beer are a potent combination so I'd soon be looking for a nice spot to unwind and catch up on the news of the day. On one such Sunday a huge oak tree that appeared to be almost growing out of a high stone wall beckoned invitingly. It was the ideal spot. I pulled into the gateway, unfolded the paper and in no time at all I was in the land of nod. Next thing I knew there was a rap on the window. Outside the car stood this huge Yorkshire farmer with hands the size of wheel rims, a craggy unshaven face and funny old hat with a large hole right in the centre of the crown. We were completely surrounded by his herd of about forty Friesian cows, and there I was, silly galoot, parked right in the driveway to his field. The gate had to open out, so I had to move. Full of apology I inched the Mini back towards the road and gave him a hand to swing open the massive cast-iron gate. It weighed a ton.

The cattle knew where to go and were soon streaming in to their favourite pasture, while the farmer and I got chatting.

'I got a brother over in Australia,' the farmer said. 'Lives near Brisbane. His name's Horace. You'd know him. Everyone knows him.'

It took some time and a map drawn in sandy soil with a dead stick to describe just how far Brisbane was from Sydney. And that it would take me as long to fly there as it would for him to fly to Germany. He couldn't believe it. There were other relations too. And I found myself scratching around in the old grey matter for the geographic locations of half of the outposts he was talking about. In the space of no more than ten minutes Arthur—'call me Arty'—and I became great mates. I had to come home and meet the family. Had to repeat the geography lesson for them. It was great. There were seven kids. And his wife didn't seem fazed by anything that went on around her. The fact that suddenly there was another place at the dinner table meant absolutely nothing. You can guess what the meal was. Roast beef and, dead right, Yorkshire Pudding. Washed down with a bit of the local ale. Tetley, if I remember correctly. And to finish off a dose of his own home-brew. Thank heavens I only took half a dose! It was a potent drop. And I think the old Mini wound her way home more through instinct than good management.

Such is the nature and generosity of country people right around the world. They take a total stranger into their home as if he were part of the family. I guess that's why my heart really lies in the country.

12

Winnie the British Bulldog

If you've never experienced the sheer joy of owning a British bulldog then I'd say you've really missed something. It's hard to remember just how old I was at the time. Seven or eight I'd guess, and my brother Neil was two and a half years my junior. My mother had always made such a big thing of the two and a half and I could never understand why. Maybe it was because the interval was almost exact, my birthday being 20 February and his 18 August.

Our home was at Linley Point on the banks of the Lane Cove River in Sydney and we lived on a fairly large block of land by today's standards. It was probably big enough to accommodate four houses—and each of those would have had a larger than average backyard as well. There were two blocks of land between us and the river itself and for the early part of our lives these had remained vacant. But finally and within a very short period of time both were sold and houses constructed.

The first resident lasted only a year or so. We didn't like him much. He was dark and swarthy and we were a bit scared of him. He sold and moved on and the place was taken over by an older couple, complete with a bulldog. Now I grew up with a father who believed that there was only one true breed of dog and that was a smooth-haired fox terrier. I remember spending many weekends with Dad at Terrier Club Shows. In fact, I think he was a foundation member of the British Terrier Club in Australia. In those days the emphasis seemed very much on the British. These were events where elderly gentlemen, dressed in crumpled grey suits and shiny black shoes, sat about on hard wooden benches for hours in deep conversation over the merits of this dog or that. Many puffed thoughtfully on blackened pipes, and even now as I think of it I can smell the nutty sweet aroma of tobacco, and feel the crispness of the straw bedding on the benches where I often used to fall asleep. I'd wake to see the understanding smile of that wonderful old man with the flowing silvery beard who was Dad's constant companion and I suspect mentor as well. I think his name was Court-Rice and perhaps he marketed the odd dog remedy or two. But I can't be sure; it's all too long ago.

At these shows only terriers were allowed to compete. And a bulldog doesn't look like any terrier I've ever seen. In fact this dog next door was the total opposite of everything and anything my father admired in a dog. Its face looked as if it had smashed headlong into a brick wall at a hundred miles an hour. Sort of like the front end of a cheap Japanese car after an argument with a fully laden concrete truck. The body was kind of broad at the front and narrow at the back. The legs were anything but straight and the tail was totally corkscrewed into a funny little stub that fitted fairly neatly onto the dog's rear end. What's more, the dog didn't know how to walk. She sort of waddled, and as she did, she grunted. In fact she never stopped grunting. Any effort at rapid movement would bring a throaty pant interspersed with a grunt, or a gasp, or a cough, or whatever noise the upper part of her respiratory anatomy seemed able to conjure up. On top of that she dribbled. And the more she smiled—and she was always smiling—the more she dribbled. 'Why,' my father asked, 'would anyone want a dog like that?'

Well, time went by as time has a habit of doing, and my brother and I began to notice that the neighbours' dog was getting fatter. But it wasn't just fat. We'd seen enough dogs to know she was pregnant. Of course, we had to have one of the pups. Poor old Dad. He didn't stand a chance. Two nagging kids and a wife who was obviously on their side, he should have given up from the word go. I can imagine what went through his mind. Fancy him, a devotee of the terrier breed, giving shelter to anything as misshapen as a British bulldog. Though there was some compensation; at least it was British.

The bitch had seven pups, I remember that much, and we often visited them as they were growing. Like little animated blobs of white blancmange they slithered around the whelping box, teetering from one side to the other on legs that could scarcely support their weight. To us they were far more interesting than any fox terrier, and isn't it a fact that children always seem to find what is going on next door far more interesting than what is going on at home. Well my brother and I kept up the pressure and Dad gave in. And y'know, I think when she arrived on the kitchen floor that night, Dad was as pleased as we were. He was without doubt the world's greatest softie, and like me he would cry at the drop of a hat. I don't think it would have mattered what young thing he'd carried home that night, he'd have been just as proud. I was amazed to find that this little pup, for all its six weeks, was a perfect replica of its mum. It waddled along with the same rear-ended, bum-swinging action. It huffed, puffed, wheezed, and snorted exactly as its mother had done. And then it piddled right in the middle of the kitchen floor. There were of course the usual arguments as to whom the dog would sleep with that night, but the family finally decided that she would sleep on the back verandah. That way arguments would be kept to a minimum.

I can't remember many problems as she grew, well nothing of note, until winter set in. Our home was a cement-rendered, very solid brick house, with a large garden that my father tended both lovingly and constantly. In those days, and I'm talking over forty years ago, things like central heating were only for the rich and famous, and believe you me, we were neither of these. We lived in the kitchen. And that's where Winnie lived too. Well, up until our bedtime at least. That's right, Winnie was her name. What else could you call a dog with such a proud British heritage and a face reminiscent of the cigar-smoking wartime leader.

Now the kitchen was heated by a kerosene-fuelled device called a 'Fyreside'. They were large cumbersome arrangements you could carry about from place to place if you wished, provided of course you'd done the mandatory six months' weight training at the local gym. They came in various colours, chocolate brown for one; ours was cream. It stood just over two feet high and was about the same in width and almost as much from front to back. The big bit at the back contained a large bottle which you filled with blue kerosene each night before turning it upside down and dropping it into what had to be exactly the right spot. But the front of the unit was where the action was. In the very centre, sticking up like some sawn-off Saturn 5 rocket, sat the burner, a pretty ugly cylindrical device with a dome on top filled with magical wires that glowed red hot when the thing was going full belt. This glorious assembly of modern science and engineering obviously had its roots in the American car industry, because the front of the apparatus was covered with more chrome than you would encounter on a 1960 Cadillac. Everything was glistening. At the back was a huge reflective dish and I suppose it was there for a purpose, to radiate the heat. But that was only part of it. The whole front assembly was chrome as well, and Mum kept it shining brightly with liberal doses of Bon Ami and elbow grease. To top it off there was a sort of grille on top where we often placed a kettle. You never knew when you might need a cuppa.

So, here we are at the start of winter and the Fyreside gets trundled out for another year. Enter one inquisitive bulldog. Now if you've ever had the chance to watch a bulldog in action, they're like most inexperienced pugilists—they lead with their chin. Well sort of. It's really the nose that comes first, probably because it's the most forward projecting part of the anatomy and always well lubricated by mountains of frothy white saliva. The other thing I reckon about bulldogs is that they're probably short-sighted. Anyway, Winnie waddled over to inspect the Fireside and was amazed to see another dog inside the apparatus. She stopped dead in her tracks, cocked her head to one side. So did her new-found friend, so Winnie stepped closer. By now her tail, or rather her whole rear end, was wagging. She threw caution to the wind and charged forward, anxious to meet this other wonderful dog that seemed just as anxious to meet her. There was a loud sizzling sound, accompanied by the smell of lamb's fry being cooked in a too hot pan that was short of oil. The chrome was fiery hot. But Winnie didn't seem to mind and went back for another close encounter, with exactly the same result. In the end, she had to be physically restrained.

◆

Now my brother and I were as devilish as most kids. And we devised a little game to keep Winnie amused. We called it 'chase the pea'. To fully understand the origins of this pastime, you have to go back to the days when peas where not bought in a frozen packet, but in pods and in pounds, not in kilos. There was always some sort of argument in the house as to who would shell the peas, and regardless of the outcome, you could bet that two or three of the little green blighters would cascade out of the colander and onto the floor.

I've already established that our Winnie was a very inquisitive dog. Everything she did was full on. So the sight of her trying to get close enough to a pea to be able to actually pick it up in her mouth was hilarious. Inch by inch she would close in on it, gently sniffing with all the stealth a bulldog can muster. The only problem was that the closer she got the more intense the sniffing became. When finally almost within gobbling range, she could control her exuberance no longer. The sniff became a snort, and the pea would be propelled forward at a rate of knots across the floor, and out of her reach. Then the whole process would start all over again. She always won in the end. Once that renegade pea hit the skirting boards, she had it covered.

My father had always pointed out that, in his experience, bulldogs tended to be very 'short in the bowel'. As a child I really never knew what that meant but believe you me, it didn't take too long to find out. A trip in the car on a Sunday with Winnie in full swing was akin to a visit to the local tannery. Boy could this dog fart! Almost on cue and with monotonous regularity. And they were explosions of the utmost frequency and intensity. We never went anywhere in the car with Winnie without having every window wound right down. We never experienced the same problem in the house however. She seemed to respect the sanctity of the kitchen. In fact I've often wondered whether her obvious anxiety in the car reflected my father's driving capabilities.

In those days the family vehicle was a 1937 Buick. Real Elliot Ness sort of stuff, but without the running boards. It was a huge thing with a straight eight motor, three-speed gear box, and it must have weighed two tons. There was nothing under the bonnet except for the radiator, motor and battery. It didn't have any indicators, but it did have bucket seats. Because of the absence of indicators you had to use hand signals, and my dad, God bless him, seemed to believe that as long as he stuck his arm out the window he could do just about anything. And there were occasions when he did. Still, we all survived.

I used to drive the old Buick from home to the university farms at Cobbitty in my final year of vet science. One day I had an argument with a guy in a Volkswagen. There was this fairly long stretch of road leading to the turn off. It was slightly up hill as well. Vision both ways was unobstructed. He was closing on us fast as we climbed the slow incline. I signalled with my right arm well in advance of the turn, yet still he kept coming. Sure enough, he overtook about halfway through my right-hand turn. Strike me lucky, I was halfway across the other side of the road. There were two thuds, but the Buick never seemed to veer off course.

'Geez! We sure collected him,' my mate sitting next to me exclaimed. And we sure had. We pulled up on the wrong side of the road and got out to check the damage. You've never seen anything like the Volksie. The front bumper of the old girl had dug into both his mudguards on the passenger side, and opened up a six-inch-wide gash in each, rolling the metal up like we used to do with a key on the lid of a sardine tin. The old girl didn't even have a scratch. The driver's side bumper was bent forward maybe half an inch, certainly no more. They don't build 'em like they used to. The towies came, the cops came, they took him away, we drove off, and were only five minutes late for our first lecture.

I have fond memories of loving, exuberant, never-know-when-to-grow-up Winnie. Will I ever get another bulldog? Perhaps yes. It's always hard to replace animals from the past, and childhood experiences are so different to those of adulthood. No, I think to have one again would cloud her memory, although on reflection Tassie certainly is the best climate in Australia for this sort of dog. Problem is, there are just so many wonderful breeds of dogs in this world of ours, I will never live long enough to experience half of the number I would wish to own.

13

Schein

At university, from about second year on, I had a job working at the local veterinary clinic. Every Saturday morning I would be on the doorstep at seven o'clock with some pretty rough working clothes. It was my job to clean the kennels which probably sounds pretty menial these days, but I did it to get experience. And I tell you what, it was the best thing I've ever done. In those days Gladesville Veterinary Clinic, as it was then known, was run by Perry Manusu and Bob Ratcliffe. They were two great vets and they were happy to have me there so long as I stayed down the back. And that was fine. My job was simply to move the dogs and the cats from one side of the kennels to the other, and clean the kennels from which they'd come. It taught me how to handle animals, the best approach, body language, injury prevention and all the things that have helped me in my years as a vet.

There was another plus to the whole exercise. Most of the animals in hospital needed some sort of veterinary attention. They were either very ill or recovering from surgery. Now the vet on duty usually rolled in about 8.30 a.m. and spent the first hour or so down in the hospital doing his rounds. I got to learn a lot about basic veterinary examination and even about some of the common disease problems that you saw in day-to-day practice.

Back in those days, around thirty-five years ago, veterinary science and the drug companies were struggling to produce compounds to treat many of the routine problems we encountered. One of these was Demodectic mange. It was a swine of a disease and still is in some dogs today. The problem is caused by a little mite that burrows into the follicle from which hair grows. Having got down there it lays eggs; these hatch into larvae and the whole process causes the follicle to eject the hair. When this occurs over a large area you get big bald patches, and in some cases nearly the whole dog can be affected. It's an interesting disease, because it appears that pups contract it from their mother at the time they begin to suckle. While they're feeding, the rotten little mites crawl off the mother and onto the pup's face or front feet. From there they can make their way over the entire body. The other peculiarity is that while most dogs tend to have some mites on their body but not enough to cause a problem, others have thousands and develop, in some cases, unresolvable problems. We think it's got a lot to do with the dog's immune system, and there's no doubt some breeds are more badly affected than others.

One Saturday when I was working, down to the hospital came two young Doberman puppies, no more than ten weeks old. They were both covered with Demodectic mange. Their poor little faces and front legs were almost totally bald. Their skin was grey and wrinkled and their eyes half-closed and full of pus. The poor little buggers were a wretched sight. They'd been on treatment from a young age but were getting worse at a rapid rate. The prognosis was so bad that it seemed both were at the end of the road. I don't know what it was about one of them. Perhaps just the way it waggled its bum, and licked my face, as I carried her into the kennels. But somehow that little pup wanted to live. Over the years I've seen many dogs at death's door, fighting for their last breath, who make it. It's called a will to live. Some have it and some don't. And by God, this dog did.

With the owner's permission this dog was mine, but I couldn't take her home. Cripes, my father would have had a stroke. It would take a week or two to prepare him for the event. In the meantime the problem was how to treat this dog when everything else had failed. I hadn't been at uni long enough to really know the ins and outs of this skin problem. But I sort of figured that if we could get the right sort of insecticide down inside the follicles where the damn things were breeding, we might stand some chance of beating the problem. Now my boss Perry had a small manufacturing company called Troy Laboratories which used to make all sorts of goodies for treating allergic skin conditions in dogs, not to mention concoctions for horses and a whole range of injectable drugs as well. They had a pretty good cupboard full of chemicals. So, with the help of their chemist and a few reference books from the uni we came up with a treatment regime.

Without going into too much detail, it involved simply this. We would treat the dog with a chemical that would remove the waxy secretions from the hair follicles first. The theory was that then the insecticide would be able to get down more easily and kill off those rotten mites. The chemicals we chose were irritant, so we had to give the pup an anaesthetic to paint the stuff on. We only did half the dog at a time, and in time it seemed to be working. A fortnight down the track and things really looked promising. By then I'd done all the ground work at home too—you know, the sort of soft-sell stuff about how if I didn't take it home it would be put to sleep. It was the line

I knew Dad would go for, without a worry.

Dad was a very keen gardener and one of his main delights was growing and breeding dahlias. For those with very little horticultural experience, dahlias are an easy flower to grow. First of all you place a tuber in the ground and then in the spring it shoots and the resulting plant is trained up a wooden stake to flower in all its glory during summer. There are many different varieties: the little ones like a round ball, called pompoms; the nymphaea, like a waterlily; the hybrid cactus; the collerette; and of course the giant decorative with a flower the size of a dinner plate. Dad kept very accurate records as he crossed one flower with another during the season. The seeds were kept and grown on in an effort to produce even better, and, in some cases, bigger blooms. My dad had a system. Every so often he would buy a sheet of flat galvanised iron and have it guillotined into long metal strips about an inch wide. He then cut these into lengths of five or six inches. When he wanted to label a particular plant he would simply dip his small finger in a can of white paint, put a small drop at one end of the metallic strip and using the heel of his hand spread the paint over the length of the strip. Then, before it had a chance to dry, he would take an indelible pencil, wet the tip with his tongue, and write in the paint. Those labels are still there now, as good as the day he wrote them, although I've often wondered since whether indelible pencils were toxic and how he managed to avoid lead poisoning from all that paint.

Do you believe in reincarnation? Well if you do, there's no doubt my Doberman puppy was a filing clerk in her previous life. I wanted to give her a German name, and I came up with Schein. We used to pronounce it Shane and everyone thought I was mad, but I liked it anyhow. By the time she came home her skin was looking so much better and you could see the hair starting to grow. Like all pups she had a mile of energy and would tear around the front lawn like some black and tan gazelle. She was a lovely dog. But it didn't take her long to discover that dahlia tubers were wonderful substitutes for balls and bones. And having been involved in the secretarial industry in her previous life, she was determined to rearrange her office—meaning my dad's garden—to suit herself. We would come home and the lawn would be littered with dahlia tubers and labels. She'd have had a wonderful time and we'd have only an hour to solve the problem before Dad got home.

Now two teenagers, quite frankly, don't know too much about dahlias. So we just got stuck in and put things back wherever we could. This went on for weeks until finally, after some consultation with our all-knowing mother, Schein was confined to the rear half of the block. Poor old Dad. Come the summer, he never really knew how to explain it. Suddenly he had dahlias that should have produced flowers the size of dinner plates producing things that looked like coloured golf balls, and vice versa. In the space of four weeks this dog had totally reorganised, or should I say destroyed, the records of some thirty years of breeding. I'll never know whether he knew the cause. We certainly didn't tell him, and he didn't ask.

Schein was my constant companion through my latter years at university and early years in practice. She had a beautiful coat and a wonderful temperament. I don't know why people are frightened of Dobermans. They really are one of the nicest dogs you could ever hope to meet. I guess some folks have just watched too many war movies. Sadly, Schein passed away while I was working in England. You never replace a dog like that. No photos do them justice; only memories can help to relive your days with them. Janine and I have had another Doberman since we moved to Tasmania. There's something special about each one of them. She was a lovely dog too, but we lost her when she returned to her breeders to have one litter for them. But that's another story, one without a happy ending. One thing's for sure the next one we get, and there will be a next one, will never leave our care.

14

Shandy

When you've been married for fifteen years to a woman who you knew for another five before that, getting to meet another lady is more than just a challenge. I'd nearly forgotten how to do it. Janine lived only about a few hundred metres down the road from my veterinary clinic in Annangrove. It was on the main road and she rented a house next to the local general store. As a matter of fact, she shared the house with a female vet who worked in a practice not too far from mine. She called me one morning when her housemate was on holidays to whip up there and look at a goat that had been badly mauled by a dog. The goat was in a real mess and unfortunately I had to put it down. I brought it home and buried it in my backyard.

I never got to meet Janine at this stage, but she told me later she was watching out the bedroom window. I know now she'd have been far too upset anyway.

Some four or five months later a very attractive young lady arrived at the door of the clinic with two fairly motley looking budgies in a little wire cage. Everyone in the district knew I had budgies. In fact, in those days, I probably had over a thousand in a massive aviary complex at the back of the house. She asked if I could give them a home. No worries, I thought. What's another two birds in with all that I've got? So of course I said yes. She was off to northern Queensland. She'd met the man of her dreams and was going to live with him on a mine site.

Wow, I thought, there is still such a thing as true love. Here am I looking at the other side of the coin.

I was feeling pretty low one night sometime later and I'm not too proud to admit that 'John Walker' was a crutch that I leant on from time to time while my world fell apart around me. The phone rang and I answered with a slur. It was some woman with a dog that she couldn't keep in, it kept jumping the fences and taking off. It had caused a couple of near misses on the road and the council had said that if she didn't do something, they would. What could I suggest? Frankly, not much. Certainly not over the phone and in the state I was in. So she brought the dog up. We would find it another home in a more rural area, I'd suggested.

I recognised her straightaway. What happened to the mine site? What happened to true love? 'You know how things don't work out sometimes,' she said.

'Yeah,' I said. 'I know. I'm looking at divorce square in the eyes.'

'Should have a cup of coffee one night and talk about it.'

'Yeah,' I said. 'Give us your phone number.'

It took me two weeks to ring but we had dinner and the rest is history. The first one left and love came back into my life.

Now some time ago, there was a song, which I think said, 'Love me, Love my Dog'. I can relate to that. It wasn't exactly an ultimatum, but it was pretty close to it. Janine moved in and so did the dog. Her name was Kushla, a giant German Shepherd, spayed female. She was a lovely dog, but fair dinkum, the damn thing lost so much hair you could stuff a mattress with it each week. But she did have a lovely way about her, a lot of pound dogs do. It's almost as though they're grateful for being given a second chance. This was Kushla's, and she had fallen on all four feet. Problem was she was old, had experienced heartworm disease, and felt the pangs of arthritis when the winter set in. I had, or rather my children had, two whippets, Pretty and Josie, that I'd bought some time earlier from a greyhound client of mine up the Hunter Valley. They were nice neat little dogs, big on looks, but short on brains. Somehow all three got on well together.

The clinic was as busy as ever and it was part of the house so the whole family tended to drift in and out as I was working. I liked that because a vet's life is pretty busy and to have your family sharing what you do is pretty nice. They were always talking to the clients and mingling with their animals. One day a nice little blue cattle pup came in for vaccination. Janine latched onto the owner. She'd always fancied a cattle dog. And you wouldn't believe it, that hand of fate again, the litter was just down the road. Didn't take her too long to zoom down and grab one. The last one—a little bitch. She called her Shandy and she was to be one of the nicest little dogs I've ever known. She never barked much. She just sort of looked at you and gave a funny sort of whinge. She only ever made three-quarter size, but was as smart as all get out, trained just so easily and loved her mum. So now there were four dogs in the backyard.

Sometimes the early part of any relationship can be put under colossal strain. Ours was. Janine drove this horrible burgundy coloured V8 Kingswood. Even to this day, when she's been forced to step backwards into a supercharged V6 she keeps telling me there's nothing like a V8. I thought, the V6 is not going to be with us for long, supercharged or not! Anyway, we used to love driving up the mountains; well, we were halfway there already. Out through Windsor and Richmond and up the Bells Line of Road to Mt Victoria. Didn't matter what time of year, it was just great to get up into the clean fresh air of the mountains. By the time Shandy had reached four months it was time to get her used to the car. Easier said than done. When we approached the foot of the first hill Shandy was in great spirits, breathing freely, nose out of the window, tail wagging, enjoying the trip. By the time we were halfway up the climb however, things had taken a turn for the worse. She was on the floor, drooling saliva, looking extremely concerned and making those funny sort of hiccuppy movements which suggested that the saliva would soon be followed by something of a more substantial nature. At the top of the hill she threw up.

I was sort of half prepared and on the second trip fully prepared. We'd pull up and, being the valiant gentleman that I am, I would walk slowly round to the passenger door, carry out this poor, limp form of canine protoplasm and stand her on the side of the road while I mopped up the sticky mess and sprayed the car with deodorant. I always carried a few spare towels in the boot from there on in.

She grew out of her carsickness in a hurry, as most dogs do, and became a seasoned traveller. She enjoyed life at Annangrove, her walks through the bush and her trips with the horses on the trails in and around the area. I think she was probably the boss of the yard. She didn't take any cheek from the others and had nothing but disdain for the litter of greyhounds that I had down the back.

As time moved on I found our Burmese cats were starting to take over a lot of my outside enclosures. We were breeding and showing very successfully. But one morning we encountered a disaster. Three cats had suddenly become paralysed, unable to walk and unable to stand. Breathing difficulty, dilated pupils and rapidly slipping off the face of the planet—snake bite. Three of our best cats dead, three of the most adventurous, probably the three that went out to play. It was a deadly game they lost.

No more than three months later I was home on my own with all the dogs and all our cats. 'The boss' was up in Queensland with an old friend. Every morning after breakfast I would go to the back door and call the dogs. They were usually there anyway on the back verandah, under the fibreglass awning, lying on their hammock beds. But not this morning. It was a very still morning. Heavy dew on the grass and the sun still barely above the horizon. No-one came when I called. There wasn't a murmur. I could see and hear nothing.

Behind the house and out to one side I had planted a peppercorn tree. It was next to the old wooden bale that I used to milk my first house cow. The tree had been slow to grow but now it was well over four metres high, spreading out and starting to throw some shade onto the grass underneath. I'd only walked half a dozen steps out the back door when I realised something was wrong. You know how you get that feeling, a sort of a knot in your stomach and a tension across your temple, that makes your heart pause for a moment. There under the peppercorn lay Shandy, still and cold but no dew on her body. Legs stretched out stiff, head arched, no breath escaped her lips. She would run no more alongside the horses, she'd yap no more at the cats, she'd ride no more with us up the mountains. Her friends sat beside her in a silent vigil. They didn't move when I called. They were doing something that was far more important; they were with their friend, standing guard, held there by some force that we can only imagine, paying their last respects. Their friend had died protecting her

118

home, for there in the grass, no more than five feet away, lay a snake. A brown snake, in three or four pieces, which when joined would have amounted to over six feet. It was huge, enough venom to kill twenty people, my friends tell me. It had taken only one bite to kill Shandy. Shandy our little friend, lies at Annangrove still. We miss you little dog, we miss you very much.

15

Ginger

Ever since becoming a vet I have had a special interest in grey-hounds. I think it dates from the very first weekend that I was on duty at the clinic. I was it, the only vet there on a Sunday. No nurse, no receptionist, no nothing, just me. There were two cars in the carpark and one of them had a greyhound sitting in the back. He was first cab off the rank, so I called him in. He was a young good-looking bloke, pretty tall with a reddish-coloured bitch on the lead. It was pretty obvious what the problem was. She had quite a deep skin wound underneath one eye. Well, I went ahead just as if it was any ordinary dog. Whacked in a local anaesthetic and sewed the thing up, while she lay quietly on the table. Now while I'm getting on with my job this bloke's going on with a constant babble about this thing being the greyhound of the year and all that sorta stuff. Quite honestly, didn't mean too much to me.

Come Monday the bosses were anxious to know how things had been, and I guess they were relieved that I hadn't totally destroyed the business during my first weekend on duty. 'It was a pretty harrowing experience,' I said to Bob. 'This bloke had come in with this dog and was giving me all this rubbish about greyhound of the year.'

'What was her name?' he asked.

'Moss,' I said. 'Something stupid about Moss.'

'Not Rose Moss?' he asked.

'Yeah,' I said, 'that's it.'

'Strike,' he said, 'she was the greyhound of the year and without a doubt one of the greatest greyhounds of all time.' Greyhound practice suddenly became a lot more important and Rose Moss raced from then on in with a slightly wicked wink in one eye.

You may recall that when my first wife and I went to England for our honeymoon I got a job as a vet in Cheshunt near Cambridge not too far out of London. The practice was essentially a small animal one but pretty close to the major greyhound kennel. Dog racing in the United Kingdom is very different to racing in Australia. While dogs are privately owned, they are trained in a huge complex by trainers who are paid by a company which you pay for the privilege. And the prize money in those days was pathetic. Anyway, I struck up a pretty close friendship with Bruce Prole, the vet of the establishment, and thought that I might take a dog or two back to Australia when I ultimately returned.

My next position was at Salisbury. This was cow country, very few dogs and even fewer cats. I spent a good deal of my spare time poring over form guides and racing magazines searching for bloodlines that I thought might offer some worthwhile investigation. At last I found one. The greyhound of the year in England was a dog called Hiver Whitenose. She was a deadset champion, a Rose Moss of England. A sensational stayer, she was by a fairly ordinary sire out of a bitch Hiver Swanky. The thing that really appealed was that two brothers from the same litter had been top grade performers as well. And funnily, they both had names like mine. One was called Happy Harry and the other Harry's Oppo. I dashed off a quick note to the breeder who replied that yes, he did have a bitch from the same litter which he would be happy to sell. We made a time, I had a look, and Ginger Lashes came home with me.

She was a big greyhound, tall and leggy, a rich red fawn with only a little white on her toes. Her form up until then was pretty patchy. She'd won a race or two, but in pretty slow time. My job back home was to make slow dogs go quick. This was a challenge. A full clinical exam, a muscle check (I'm a part-time chiropractor as well), a blood sample and I thought we should have some answers. Next door to the practice was a laboratory with what I presumed was pretty up-to-date equipment. Alas and alack, this was not to be the case. Now this lab, next door, was next to useless. Quite honestly if they were presented with anything more than a dead chook it seemed beyond them. So down to the local hospital I went, a few words in the right place and the local pathologist and I are running Ginger's blood through the lab. Now to say that things were a little antiquated in English veterinary practice some thirty years ago would be absolutely dead accurate. Ginger had hookworms, even though all the vets told me they didn't have hookworms here. Well, you better come and look down the microscope because this must be the first case! There was nothing to treat them with, had to import it from America.

To race a dog on a track in England they have to qualify. This means running a time that is sufficiently fast for that particular track. Ginger had been racing only on low grade tracks. She'll never make it at White City, the premier track, I was told. But then nobody tells Ginger that sort of thing. She lived in kennels at the back of the practice at Salisbury and we trained her on the local common. I would walk her in the morning and my wife would walk her at night.

I'd also purchased a broken-down bitch to add to the collection. She'd had a major injury that prevented further racing. But her blood lines were sound and I thought her worth a try as a brood bitch. One particular afternoon I came back from work to find my wife really distressed. The dogs were back in the kennels early and she was in tears. It turned out that she had been walking in her usual place when this guy rolls up with half a dozen Pekinese and just proceeds to let them run all over the place. She couldn't control our dogs and brought them home. The park regulations required all dogs to be on a lead and she told him so but he slung off about our colonial breeding and took no notice.

Next afternoon, it was my turn. I walked into the park and there he was with his little Pekinese dashing here and dashing there. Now don't get me wrong, I like all dogs. Well most of them. But if you're going to own a dog then you need to obey the rules. And the rules said: 'All Dogs Must be on a Lead'. Mine were on leads and they had muzzles too. I yelled out for him to get his on a lead, please. And he replied, in a fairly broad Wiltshire dialect, that he had no intention of doing that and again reflected on my ancestry. 'Well,' I said, 'if it's good enough for your dogs, it's good enough for mine too.'

And with that I tightened up the muzzles and undid the collar on both bitches. I didn't think Pekes were terribly quick, but by cripes they moved that afternoon. They seemed to be moving in three directions at once and if they could've climbed trees they'd have done that too. Funnily enough, we never had any more trouble. In fact we never saw him again and quite frankly I'm sure my two girls didn't really do any harm. Rules are for everybody!

I took Ginger down to the greyhound kennels near the first

practice where I'd worked. She was reasonably fit but needed a little more galloping. Did she qualify? She qualified at her first go. Slashed the time by nearly 0.4 of a second. Not a bad effort for a dog that was only an also-ran up until then.

I only ever saw her race once. It was just before we were due to come back home. Rabies had struck the United Kingdom and all my plans about bringing her back on the boat with us had to be abandoned. I took a mate to the race. He was an Aussie over there on holidays just like us. I didn't have too much of the folding stuff left and it was going to be a long trip home by boat. It was Christmas Eve, Race 2. She'd drawn the number four box. I was at great lengths to explain to my mate that in England they only race six dogs at a time, whereas back home we had a field of eight. Now those who know me well, and even those who don't, realise that I wear glasses. They were due for a change, so when the dogs jumped from the boxes and ran away from me around the first corner I yelled to him, 'Who's in front?' He said it was the dog with the black rug.

I said, 'That's the seven.'

'Hang on a minute,' he said, 'aren't there only six dogs in the field?'

Struth, I had to whip open the race book and see which box carried the black rug. It was the four. You bloody beauty. She bolted in by six lengths—we got twelve to one. What a fabulous trip home.

All up, Ginger was to win twenty-three races for us in the United Kingdom before coming to Australia. She was of course too old to race when she got here but as I'd bought her for breeding anyhow, I guess it didn't really matter.

♦

It was the holiday weekend in January way back in 1975 when I got a message that a fire was coming up the gully behind our house. Over twenty of my greyhounds were burnt to death. Those that remained alive included a litter of six pups. Their mother had died on top of them, and they seemed dazed, totally unable to cope with the situation. I was pretty much the same way myself, although the sight of so many animals charred beyond recognition is something that time eventually erases. I started to look around for those animals that were special and of course, the one dog I couldn't find was Ginger. Her kennel door was open. (The neighbour had managed to let some dogs out before the fire struck.) But she was nowhere to be seen.

An hour or so later the family arrived and we sat around counting our losses and speculating on what could have been and what should be. I sat on the front verandah with the acrid smell of smoke in the air, I looked up the drive and there walking down were two little girls. Between them they had a red dog, just on a piece of string. As they got closer that familiar walk, the high tail carriage and those dark brown eyes seemed to say, 'I'm okay, I was frightened, but I'm all right now.' Ginger walked up to me and the tears were rolling down my face. She started to lick and kept licking and the more she licked the more I cried. I hugged her and I kissed her. My Ging was alive and somehow that gave new hope.

It seems that she had fled in panic, and who wouldn't blame her. What can prepare an animal for an onslaught such as this? Unlike us, they are rarely conditioned by a previous experience. We know what fire means, and we know what fire does. An animal who has never experienced such an event often doesn't know how to react, and yet that fight or flight instinct still told Ging she should run. And run she did, hiding in the next-door neighbour's garage. They'd shut the door, not knowing she was inside and fled themselves. Their house and their garage and Ginger all survived. But it wasn't until they got home that they realised what had happened.

We rebuilt everything, put in a swimming pool, a pump and a generator. We will never be caught again. Most of Ginger's pups were lost in that fire. Those that survived never raced, their lungs far too badly damaged by the heat and the smoke of that awful day. She did have other litters and one in particular was very successful. At the age of eleven Ginger passed away. Greyhounds are not long lived. I have all her papers and her race results filed away. She was my favourite, she was the best, and she always will be.

16

Easy Pickens

Greyhounds had been my passion for quite a number of years. I enjoy the breed and the racing. They are the perfect performance machine. And quite honestly, so much better than horses. (Hope my wife doesn't read that.) I mean, you walk into a stable, you spend two hours grooming and polishing a horse, and if you're unlucky you get a boot in the backside as you walk out the door. Your dog starts barking at four o'clock in the morning, you get up and abuse it, maybe even throw something in its general direction, then at six o'clock when it's walk time, you are greeted like a long-lost friend.

A young couple from Newcastle had become regular clients and good friends too. His name was Ian, hers was Jan. They'd had a dog or two in years past with only average ability. But this time they rolled up with a pup. Well not quite a pup. He was about fourteen months old and there was quite a story to him. It seems they had two dogs being reared on an establishment in the Hunter Valley. Now, something mysterious had gone wrong with these two pups. No-one quite knows, or was prepared to admit, what actually happened. Whether disease, accident or poison no-one would say. But both of them met an early end. The proprietor was good enough to offer them a replacement—which did suggest to me that perhaps he felt just a trifle responsible for what had gone on. Anyway, this was that dog.

He was a light fawn, skinny-looking individual and seemed very unsure of himself as they hoisted him onto the table. They wanted the once-over and that's what he got. A bit dehydrated, dull and dry in the coat, probably half a kilo underweight, chest sounds good, no sign of tonsillitis or anything wrong in that area. A quick listen to the heart. Wait a minute. This dog had one of the slowest heart rates I had ever heard. Forty-six beats per minute, two slower than I'd ever encountered. I looked at them and chewed for a moment on the earpiece of the stethoscope. 'This dog's a bloody champion,' I said. And left the room to get a couple of blood tubes. No examination was complete without a full blood count. This would show up things that a clinical examination might miss. I collected the sample, sent them home and put it through the lab.

The dog was duly educated and even at an early stage began to show exceptional speed. He did almost as I'd predicted. Easy Pickens went on to win race after race in near-record time and then suddenly at two and a half years of age he hit a brick wall. I saw him again and the news was grim. He had a very heavy infestation of heartworm. All of this was many years ago and as vets we didn't recognise the problem that had obviously existed in so many areas of New South Wales. We'd thought it was a tropical disease, spread by mosquitoes. We were half right; it was spread by mosquitoes, and if the right ones were there so was the disease. Treatment was dangerous to say the least. Imagine a heart full of some hundred or more worms each like a thin piece of vermicelli and nearly ten inches long. Not only in the heart but in the arteries leading to the lungs as well. We can kill them all right with arsenic. But when they're dead, where do they go? Only one place—into the lungs. And if they leave in big enough numbers then they'll block a major blood vessel causing an embolus (clot) and a dead dog. We treated him and he nearly died. He got, in fact, a massive clot in one lung. How he survived I'll never know. But some animals do have that will to live and to win and to race again. He was one of those.

I reckon Easy Pickens lost around thirty per cent of one lung. Can you imagine trying to race in the very best company with a heart severely damaged by disease and with one lung very much down on capacity. He did. And he kept on winning. Without the heartworm, I reckon he could've been one of the greatest dogs of all time. But time caught up with him and he never quite made it.

Some years later we got together again, just the three of us. Easy Pickens wasn't with us anymore but we talked about old times. Ian confessed that on their visit way back then he'd quietly said to Jan, 'Harry's lost his marbles. How could he possibly know this dog is going to be a champion?' Well, it was based on a little bit of experience and a fair whack of scientific knowledge. If only I could be so lucky picking my own dogs.

That day, Ian went on to tell a story which I'll relate to you all. It seems that he had never had a great love of dogs in his early years. But in the highlands of Scotland from which they both came, when you went courting you invariably went to the home of your intended. His first visit to Jan's home was not without incident. It was a freezing night and there he sat at one end of the lounge room, almost enfolded by a huge armchair, in front of a roaring fire. At the other end of the room sat her father, a giant of a man with huge hands, a pipe and a shock of striking red hair. 'You know how it is,' said Ian, 'when you feel that sort of grumbling sensation down low in your abdomen that says there's something going on down there and eventually that something has got to come out.' He had another whisky and didn't know whether it was the grog or the fire or the tension in the cheeks of his rear that was causing his face to glow a ruddy crimson. Things got worse. And the more he strained and the more he clenched the more determined this bubble of chemical energy was to escape into the atmosphere. It's a physical fact that eventually muscles when they're kept under constant spasm have a tendency to relax of their own device. Try holding a five cent piece between your thumb and finger for any longer than ten minutes while you're walking down the road.

Anyway, physiology won over and so did the vapour. Ian sat there in the chair as mute as could be while the noxious combination of indole and skatole, two gases known to frequently inhabit the lower reaches of the bowel rose slowly into the heavy atmosphere of the lounge room. One would suspect that the chemical structure of such materials would prevent them rising above a certain height in a room with a fairly low ceiling anyhow, and that, of course, is exactly what they did. They spread horizontally across the room, almost as if drawn towards his prospective father-in-law. He put down the pipe, paused, sniffed the air, and rose slowly to his feet. Without uttering one word, this giant of a man walked slowly and purposefully towards the hapless figure now fighting back yet another explosion, right up to Ian's chair. He bent over the small cringing figure huddling on the velveteen covers. Then he reached down slowly, almost in a premeditated movement, to grasp not Ian but what lay at his feet.

'You rotten mongrel,' he said, picking up the poor little Jack Russell terrier by the scruff of the neck. He opened the door and ushered the dog outside with the toe of his boot. Ian told me he never went around to Jan's place again without taking the biggest, meatiest, juiciest bone he could possibly find. If ever a man needed a dog, he did that day.

17

Greyhounds and Glory

Greyhound racing in Ireland is a national institution. It's the only country in the world I know of where they've erected a statue to a greyhound. The dog's name was Master McGrath and he was the only greyhound to win the Waterloo Cup three times: February 1868, February 1869, February 1871. A black and white dog, the property of Lord Lurgan, weight about 54 pounds. They called him the Mighty Black. His statue stands down near Dungarvan in southern Ireland. In thirty-seven starts he only lost once.

He was a coursing dog, and in those days the sport was extremely popular. It still exists today but has been banned in many countries of the world. I've seen it. And having spent a day on the fields of Cashell under the shadows of that imposing rock fortress I learnt a lot and came away with a different view. On that day, there I was, covered in cameras like an American tourist. Telephoto lenses and the lot. They thought I was from the anti-blood sports league until I explained that I was actually a vet from Australia who spent a lot of time looking after the same breed back home.

I will describe what happens because I think it's important in life to have a balanced picture. Yes, two dogs do chase a live hare. One dog wears a white collar and one dog a red. The hares have been trained for months to run from one end of the field to the other. Only the best and fittest hares are kept and the organisers seem to spend a lot more time looking after the hares than do the owners their dogs. Down the far end stands the slipper. He is the bloke in real control of the situation. He stands with the two dogs on special leads, holding their hind legs off the ground. The hare runs down a long, narrow pathway lined with bales of straw, out past the dogs and down the field. The slipper only releases the dogs when the hare is running fast and true. It has a minimum of fifty metres start.

During the whole day I only saw two hares caught by the dogs, out of one hundred and forty-four events. And the reaction of the people standing on the hill watching the events amazed me. As soon as it became obvious that the course would end in such a manner, they would as one turn away and look up the hill. Nobody watched, nobody spoke, it was as though everybody just turned off. And it was a good five minutes before they turned back round again. Even when the events were in full swing it was the hare they were barracking for. 'Go hare', 'What a good hare', never mind the damn dog. It was a fascinating day and something you don't forget in a hurry. Everyone involved had to pose for a picture. The guys with the hares, the slipper, and the judge seated on his thoroughbred halfway down the field with a red handkerchief and a white handkerchief tucked up his sleeves which he used to convey the winner of each course to the officials. There were bookmakers, timekeepers, and all manner of very suspicious-looking individuals lurking around the place. But I was made to feel so much at home, as only the Irish can.

That's the old form of racing. Today the dogs chase a mech-anical lure around a circular track—so-called tin hare racing. Ireland has tracks everywhere and I was determined to have a good look at as many as possible. They varied from the very modern to the absolutely antiquated. I can usually get a good feel for the track and its layout by squeezing through one of the gates or grabbing a caretaker who just happens to be hanging around. On occasions, the track was in operation when I arrived. And there were nights when I actually got to attend a race meeting. Galway was one of those.

It was a Charity Night. And that meant that half the prize money from each race was donated to a local charity. I rolled up about an hour or so before the first race, introduced myself to the committee and was immediately taken on board as a long-lost friend. The vet on duty was a really affable guy. He had big bushy eyebrows, a podgy red face, and a huge nose with a large pigmented growth down near the tip which sprouted at least two or three black hairs. (I'm terrible, I seem to notice this sort of abnormality on people that I meet all the time, and then can never understand why in God's name they haven't done something about it. Are all vets the same?) Anyhow, they were all fond of a drink, and I don't mind one myself. But the vet, he had a better capacity than anyone on the committee and that included the president of the club. By the start of the first race everybody was primed for a good night.

The greyhounds are paraded on the track with their rugs corresponding in number and colour to the boxes from which they start. The most frequently travelled distance is about five hundred metres. In Ireland it was the vet's job to walk behind this gaggle of dogs as they made their way out onto the track. Just to keep an eye on things, so to speak. Everything went exactly according to Hoyle. There were no injuries and no need for intervention until the fifth race.

'Doctor Cooper, Doctor Cooper. Would Doctor Cooper kindly come to the Steward's office,' blurted the loudspeaker system, with that beautiful Irish drawl. What did they want with me? The office seemed to be in a state of panic. 'Doctor Cooper,' said the Chairman of Stewards, 'could you be takin' over the meetin' for da rest o'da night?'

'Sure,' I said. 'What's wrong?'

'Oh,' they said, 'it's Doctor O'Sullivan. He's not at all well.'

The Irish are renowned for their understatements. For there, behind the starting boxes, out cold, was Dr O'Sullivan. It really doesn't look too good for the veterinary profession to be a little inebriated when they're on the job. But when you're lay-down-grab-the-grass drunk I don't s'pose you care much anyway. Four of us picked him up, two at the front, two at the back and carried him pretty unceremoniously the whole length of the straight into the kennels where we laid him out on the floor. And there, my dear friends, he spent the rest of the charity meeting, while yours truly took over the veterinary side of things. I had one of the best nights of my life. Tell you what, Ireland's a great place.

Saddling Up

18

Horsing Around

My wife Janine is mad keen on horses. She's never been any different. Even as a kid she spent her holidays on the South Coast of New South Wales trying desperately to catch and ride some of the wild ponies that wandered backwards and forwards in the heathland behind the beach. I don't know what it is that attracts women to horses, but it is a pretty common fact that there are far more females interested in riding than there are males. So really, when we got married it wasn't just a question of love me love my dog, it was more a case of the dog, the cat and the horse.

Janine had more or less grown up with a palomino and white pinto gelding she called Coco. For those of you not quite sure what a gelding is then let me set you straight. A gelding is a desexed male. He was a really funny sorta horse that stood about fifteen hands high, and absolutely hated men. (While I'm at the technical stuff, a horse's height is always measured in hands, and a hand is about ten centimetres. The measurement is made at the horse's wither, the area just in front of the top of the shoulder blades. Phew.) If I walked into the paddock where he was grazing, he would automatically turn his rear end towards me. Didn't matter how carefully I tried to approach I was always greeted with the blunt end. Not that he meant any harm. I don't think he knew how to kick. He'd just had a lot of bad experiences growing up.

The old fella was born up the Hunter Valley, and was by a teaser stallion on a thoroughbred stud, out of a stock horse mare. (A teaser is generally a pony stallion used to test when the thoroughbred mares are properly in season and ready to mate with the chosen stallion.) He could barrel race like you wouldn't believe. All the kids, not only ours but the neighbours too, learnt to ride on our Coco. We'd made a pilgrimage early in our marriage to Raleigh on the North Coast of New South Wales to see an old mate of mine by the name of Roley. He was my mentor in so many areas. One of the original Barnardo Boys, this Pommie-turned-Aussie had made a reputation for himself as one of the most progressive farmers in the district, always willing to try new things and experiment with products and procedures he'd read about overseas. It's a shame there weren't a lot more like him. His wife, Lesley, was heavily involved in breeding ponies, and that of course was the purpose of our visit: to buy a pony to suit the kids. Crickette was that pony—and we bought her son too, a cheeky young lad by the name of Firefly.

It was quite a trip I remember, my first-ever experience at towing a horse float. Right from the beginning I wasn't all that sure about this horse business. After all, as a vet I'd soon come to realise that all horses were, quite frankly, accidents just waiting to happen. And then there was that bumper sticker that all the horsey people had: 'Poverty is owning a horse'. How right they all were. Why did we need two? After all, there was only going to be one child riding? Ah yes, Janine assured me, but in time there would be others and in any case he was quite a bargain. I'm always out talked by a woman and of course, as we had a double horse float, why not? They would keep each other company wouldn't they? Of course they would.

Beaten before I started, and so the two ponies arrived back home at Annangrove.

Crickette was a registered Australian pony but it soon became pretty obvious to all concerned that whilst she may be a bomb-proof mount for the kids, she was just never going to make it in the show ring. What was needed was a little more class, a little more presence, a little more style, and a little more pizzazz. Now not too far away from Annangrove lived Lyn Holweck, a lovely lady who had probably the leading Australian pony stud at the time. We became frequent visitors to the property at Vinegar Hill and spent many afternoons walking, talking and learning about Australian ponies.

Ultimately, we purchased two grey mares, Amberluka and Gipsy. There was plenty of room and plenty of feed at Annangrove. Since the days of that terrible fire, the back part of the property had been cleared and fenced, grass had been sown and the whole place regularly fertilised. Water was freely available and the recirculation system from the old septic tank did wonders for the pasture. There was so much grass that at one stage we even agisted some of Lyn's horses at our place. When the time came to move to Tassie, Gipsy and Amberluka were the first on the float. Boy was that a trip and a half. All in all I think we moved eight horses. Quite an effort, and as we loaded them onto the huge horse transport standing in our driveway that night, we both hoped and prayed they'd get there safely—and of course they did. As a matter of fact they beat us to Tassie by two weeks, but that's another story!

At Mole Creek in Tassie's north there was plenty of room on the six hundred acres for the horses to really enjoy life. And for the first couple of years on the farm we did too. Then, of course, the crunch came, as it did for so many farmers around

Australia. Ah yes, the Recession we had to have. Things were tough, and I mean tough, and isn't it always the fact that in circumstances such as these you're presented with a golden opportunity and quite frankly you just can't afford to do a thing about it.

In the mail came a letter and a catalogue from Vinegar Hill back home. Lyn was having a clearing sale and most of her stock were on offer. There were some fabulously bred horses, yearlings, two-year-olds, mature stock and brood mares. Janine drooled quietly over the lots on offer. But they were near Kellyville west of Sydney and we were doing it tough in Mole Creek.

'We can't even look at anything like this,' I said. But somehow we did manage to cobble a few bob together, sold some old ewes, leased out some equipment and the wool cheque came in, not that it was much to write home about! I put a limit on things and we scanned the horses on offer in detail. There were two very promising youngsters out of probably the best lines on the property. They were sure to bring a lot of money but then they were worth it. We put in a phone call to our old mate Graham Murphy, at his renowned saddlery in Dural, deposited the money in his account, and gave him authority to bid on our behalf at the sale. We knew Graham well. He was a good friend, a great saddler, and a good judge of horses. He ended up with our 'Tony the Pony', but then that's another story.

The day arrived, the sale began. We waited anxiously at home for Graham's phone call to find out what had happened. Strike a light, the two youngsters Janine wanted to buy both opened the bidding well above what we were prepared to pay. Ah well, you can't win them all. But then I'd marked one horse in the catalogue for whom I'd always had a soft spot, just in case this sort of thing happened. In life you always need to have a reserve to fall back on, and this was my reserve.

Every time we visited the stud a big black-brown mare always caught my eye. She was big, maybe even a bit too big for her type, with a huge flowing mane and forelock, good solid legs, wide dark eyes and great breadth of face. She stood tall alongside the other horses. Not only that, she moved like a machine. Only one problem, no-one could get near her! It took five people just to catch and worm her! She was the greatest headache in the whole joint. Well guess what? Graham bought her. Her name was Michelle. She was no spring chicken, born 7 November 1976, but there was something about this horse that I really liked. How do you explain that sorta thing? I don't know. I just know that every time I walked into the place she seemed to be looking at me. Lyn knew that too, and there was more than one occasion when I let her know that I really fancied this old girl in spite of her reputation. Perhaps it was fate. Who knows? Graham had a few bob left so he bought another brood mare as well. A bay roan called Moonstar. At least I was happy, even if Janine was disappointed.

It was a day or two after the sale before that wife of mine rang just to find out from the horse's mouth, so to speak, how things had gone. It had been a great sale, Lyn told her. Most of the stock that was on offer had been sold. Janine asked in detail about horse after horse. And when she'd finished it was Lyn's turn.

'Graham Murphy was here,' she said, 'and he bought two mares.'

'Oh yeah,' said Janine. 'Which two?'

'Michelle and Moonstar,' she said. 'And he wouldn't tell me who he'd bought them for. It's a shame,' she went on, 'Harry always liked Michelle, and I'd hoped that one day he might end up with her.'

'Well,' said Janine, 'he has.'

I think they both shed a few tears, but happy ones, at that. Graham had been sworn to secrecy. Lyn offered a free service to her top stallion, and both mares were put in foal and floated down to Tassie. (And I don't mean on a barge! This is horsey talk.)

By the time they were due to arrive we'd sold the Mole Creek farm and were renting a small place while we worked out where we should resettle. So what to do with the horses? By now there were quite a few more than when we started. Well initially we agisted the pair of them at a local thoroughbred stud until we could lease a paddock nearby for all the horses. There are times in your life when you need friends. And we found one. His name was Geoff Elmer. You wouldn't wish to find a nicer guy. The paddock was near his farm and he and the pair of us kept a good eye on all our stock until the next move. Some six weeks after arriving Moonstar became terribly ill. She was stabled in Geoff's barn for over a month on twice-daily antibiotics and supportive treatment. How she lived I'll never know—and she was in foal at the time as well. At one stage she went for nine days without eating more than a couple of handfuls of feed a day. Sure says a lot for the stuff ponies are made of.

Both mares foaled before we moved to the Launceston area. (We had to be closer to town and the airport because television now took up so much of my time.) Michelle had a stunning chestnut colt. He shone like the sun as it sets over the Great Western Tiers on a warm and glowing afternoon in February. Orange and yellow, scarlet and vermilion. He was like the sun on fire. We called him Sunset Fire. Sunny for short. He grew up a little bit like his mum. A pushy horse, no real malice in him at all, but really liked to get his own way and if you were standing in it, then sorry brother, you got pushed aside. From a young age he had class. If there's something about an animal that's good, I reckon they know it! They hold themselves differently, they've got a presence, and a 'look at me' attitude about them. Sunny had all of those.

One particular event sticks in my mind. It was dark and I was feeding out after work, because having to fit in both veterinary practice and television commitments was starting to take its toll. Sunny was out running in the laneway and probably about seven or eight months old at the time. It's often hard to tell what happens. It's all over so quickly. But one minute the wheelbarrow and I were travelling along the laneway and the next Sunny rushed past and up-ended me and the barrow. There I was, lying on the ground with the shafts of the barrow somehow tangled around my legs and one of his legs caught too. Most horses would have kicked out wildly. If he had, my head may look somewhat different, but he didn't. We spoke quietly while the mess was untangled and he never moved a muscle. He was a special animal, he was something else.

Sunny was a registered Australian pony and a saddle pony and as such we showed him with great success. He went on to win just about everything he possibly could in Tassie. They called him 'the little red pony with the great big trot'. You see for a small horse he moved like a big'un. He was a pleasure to ride and a pleasure to handle, except when confronted by a mare on heat. It then became more of a case of barefoot waterskiing than anything else. He was one very strong horse. Lack of opportunities at stud, simply because Tasmania is a very small place, meant that eventually we gelded Sunny and sold him. Somehow, he's never quite achieved the same successes since. Perhaps this was his home, we and Nigel and Craig who handled him were his friends. It does make a difference.

So what about ol' Michelle? She's still going and almost twenty-four years old. At the moment she's running with George our riding pony stallion. And talk about laugh, just the other morning I was feeding out. Now mostly we use meadow hay that we grow ourselves. But I like to give the stallions and the youngsters a bit extra. So I pitched in a bit of lucerne as well. There are about eight paddocks to feed and Michelle was somewhere near the middle. I'm on my way back with an almost empty trailer, and there she is, cheeky old lady, standing guard over the lucerne hay I'd thrown in to George. Every time he came near, she'd let drive with both hind legs, defiant old girl. She's a horse with a lot of history. Nearly every foal she's produced has gone on to be a Best in Show. Sunny was no exception and the three she's had for us since will emulate his example. These days she's much better behaved. The two of us can walk up to her in a paddock, hold out a bucket of feed, whisper sweet nothings in her ear, and worm her without a worry in the world.

Animals are like people; there are many that pass through your life. For some you have only a momentary glance, for others a longer look, and for the special few a transfixing stare. For all her years Michelle still has that magic. She stands tall amongst the mares and guards her foals with all the cunning she can muster. That coat still fairly glows; the mane we need to trim or it just gets too long; and the tail, well it's just so thick it's incredible. Of all the horses she is my favourite. She may not have cost the money that many have, but just to hang over that fence on a summer's day and see a chestnut foal wheeling and turning all over the paddock while she stands there proud as can be with her new offspring is worth all the dollars in the world. She'll never leave, this is her home and she'll be with us for as long as the Keeper of All Things allows her to stay.

19

Mulga Bill

Never do things on impulse. Never, ever do things on impulse. We did once, and boy did I live to regret it. It was a long time ago and I can't remember exactly in which order the whole thing came about but I think it was this way. Janine and I had talked for some time, before our marriage, about the possibilities of doing some driving. Now I don't mean behind the steering wheel of a thundering V8 or something similar, I mean real driving. Sitting there in a two-wheeled contraption, while in front of you a proud steed pulls the whole ensemble down the road. Sounds too good to be true. But then if you've seen me on a horse, then the definition of riding is hanging on, looking awkward and not falling off. So, as you can see, the thought of pleasure driving did have some appeal.

As a young veterinary student you were required to spend time with various animals throughout the course. I'd always lived in the city and while I felt pretty much at ease with cats, dogs, and birds, the larger animals were more than just a little foreign. I didn't mind cows, or sheep, but quite honestly, I was more than a little apprehensive around horses, for I'd had virtually no contact whatever with them. And don't they know just exactly how you feel about them. Of all the animals I've dealt with over the years, the horse is the best 'reader' of your awareness than any other. You see we give off what are called pheromones. They're complex chemicals that reflect how we feel about what's happening around us. They're on our breath and on our skin. Animals can read these like a lie detector machine. Just watch a horse when you walk near. The first thing it'll do is to dilate those nostrils. Then it'll take in a good few breaths of the surrounding atmosphere, analyse things and come up with a result. Almost instantly it knows exactly what you're feeling.

My father in his wisdom decided that there was only one way to conquer this problem and overcome what was, quite frankly, a fear of horses. To him, getting a job working with them—that made sense. Dad had mates just about everywhere; he was one of those men who made friends very easily—and kept them too. Anyway, contacts were made and in no time at all there I was with Les Chant and Chris Hartney working with the animal that I was to grow to respect and admire. I worked every morning in third and fourth year at Harold Park Paceway. It was very close to the veterinary faculty and there was time to put in a couple of hours before lectures. I learnt to harness and unharness trotters in my sleep. I learnt to wash them down, scrape them off, handle, lead and shoe them. I learnt plenty from the farrier too, including how to swear.

One day there we were in the shoeing shed, which was located at the very top of the stable area, on a slope behind the actual racetrack. The whole area had been excavated and as a result the roof was level with the footpath above. The horse in question this particular day was a very jumpy two-year-old colt. It was great to watch a master at work, cutting and shaping the shoes from bare metal and second-hand coil springs. It's a trade which, thank heavens, has been preserved today. These fellas are farriers, not blacksmiths; they know how to shoe horses in order to correct problems in their action, how to

149

shape and weight shoes to produce just the right length of stride. They have learnt from the best teacher of all; experience.

Les'd sweat and strain over the forge, hammering and shaping the orange glowing metal, pumping the massive bellows to gain even more heat as he perfected each 'slipper'. The heat from the fire dried the perspiration as it rolled down his forehead, but the torrents of sweat rolled down his chest and disappeared under the thick leather apron slung tightly around his waist. He was a giant of a man. Must have been a good eighteen or nineteen stone.

We were on the last leg, the right hind foot, and it hadn't been easy. It was only the second time this colt had been shod and he was pretty jumpy. It is always great to watch a real master at work, measuring the blows of the hammer to the pull and tug of the horse's leg held firmly between his massive thighs. Anyway, school holidays were in full swing and well, kids have to be kids, don't they? I mean we all went through it. Back Les comes from the forge with the glowing red shoe held firmly by the spike driven through the nail hole. Down it comes on the hoof to burn a neat ring in which to sit. It's called hot shoeing. There's a terrible smell, a cloud of acrid smoke, and a noise of burning and crackling as the shoe seats itself onto the hoof.

Now at the very time Les lifted the still glowing shoe from the hoof, there was a sudden, sharp clatter of rocks on the roof of the shed. It made a deafening din inside the building and echoed around the tin walls like a machine gun. To the horse it must have sounded like all hell had broken loose—and that's exactly the way the colt reacted. Up in the air he went and me with him, hanging on for dear life. Kicking out with both hind legs, he caught Les offguard and drove the red hot shoe straight into his side. For a big man he could move pretty quickly, I can tell you. The shoe crashed to the floor, Les grabbed a weapon from the anvil, spun around in an instant and was gone out the door and up the ramp behind the shed. Now, blacksmiths can swear, we all know that. It's their stock in trade. But Les was a master, and he was into it even before he cleared the doorway, in hot pursuit of the kids who were still laughing and chuckling about the ruckus they'd created below. As he ran, he swore, and boy oh boy did he swear. It was the greatest education in the Australian vernacular I've ever had. All this time he was waving a set of clinchers, threatening to brain the first kid he got hold of. I think he was actually gaining on them for a while, but like most blokes of his size, he only had a short sprint and the kids won the day. He swore, I reckon, for five minutes flat. He never stopped for a breath and never used the same word twice. Boy what an experience! It took an hour to calm the horse, the farrier and myself, but we did get the job done.

During this time I even got to do a bit of track work. And it's great. Sitting back in the sulky with the horse ambling along in front, reins in your hand, the air in your face and on a wet morning a fair amount of mud and grit from the track as well. I reckon I could handle driving, particularly if it were just a little pony, I thought. And then one day fate stepped in. There on the front page of a national horse magazine was an advertisement for a little harness pony. His name was Thorpeville Baledon, and he came from Myrtleford, down in northern Victoria, fairly near the snow country. He wasn't a big guy, as I recollect, only twelve and half hands, a chocolate chestnut colour but with a really appealing little face. Janine was convinced that this was the horse for us, and we hadn't even laid eyes on him in the flesh yet!

Coincidences do occur because that very same weekend, on the main road leading to Castle Hill, stood a brightly painted sulky just waiting for someone to purchase it. It was red and yellow with traditional wooden spoked wheels and polished wooden shafts. The seat was only vinyl, but it looked like leather, nut brown and shining in the afternoon sun. We happened along, on our way home from a visit to some friends nearby. And yes folks, we bought it. As a matter of fact, we bought both. The horse and the sulky.

It was a fair trip down south to Myrtleford to buy the horse. We arrived at a quaint little farm, but there he stood in the front paddock, as cute as you like, almost as if he were waiting for us to arrive. For Janine it was love at first sight. Even today I have to admit he was a very showy little horse. His owners were only too happy to harness up the little fella for us so we could take a test drive around their back paddock. He never missed a beat, and it felt good to be sitting back in the cart again whilst he trotted away out in front. Mind you, he was somewhat smaller than those trotters from some twenty or so years ago. Nonetheless, I had a few lessons on the harnessing set-up as well, before we brought the little horse home.

A lot of equipment is needed when you're going to do some driving and the harness can cost an arm and a leg. We weren't sure how far we were going to go with this particular interest, so we opted for pretty much run-of-the-mill gear. Mind you, we're still talking around four figures, but the really schmick stuff can cost up to four times that. Then again, you had to buy the right size to suit the horse. It took probably a month to get everything fully organised. We decided the best thing to do was to float the horse, the sulky, and us up the mountains somewhere, find a deserted road, and do a bit of practising. Quite honestly, we didn't have the room at home in Annangrove to undertake any real test.

The trip up was a breeze, and we found the ideal spot: a long straight sandy road with scrub on either side and not a car to be seen. It takes a while to harness a horse, attach the sulky and climb on board, and on top of this, little Tony, as he came to be known, had done nothing since arriving at our place except eat. Boy was he raring to go! Finally all the gear was attached and we backed our new-found love in between the shafts and finished the job. He looked sensational. I climbed on board, Janine opted to watch from the sidelines, and away we went. Everything seemed to be going well. He took off at a slow walk. I could handle that. My young son was riding shotgun at the time and after a hundred yards or so I clicked the pony up a bit. He broke into a collected trot. I was beginning to feel very confident. But then pride always comes before a fall.

It all happened so quickly, it's hard to recall exactly what the problem was. However I think it went something like this. The road was sandy, but there were areas where the sand was particularly deep and soft. We hit one of those areas with the right wheel of the sulky. It dug in and twisted the thing sideways. I think the shaft dug into Tony's side and he panicked. But he wasn't the only one panicking. Away we went, like an out-of-control dodgem. Didn't seem to matter what I did, I couldn't pull him up. You feel so helpless, the only thing between you and the horse are these huge long reins. Now he was galloping, full tilt, straight down the middle of the road, and the sulky was lurching dangerously in and out of the potholes. It tipped to the side. 'Bail out,' I yelled. And that's what the youngster did, right out the back. I wasn't far behind. All control was lost and the horse was in panic mode. The sulky tipped sideways again, at an angle of almost forty-five degrees, surely it must tip right over. Then we hit a rock right in the middle of the road and I was gone, out of the seat and over the side, landing on the ground 'like a bloody great sack of potatoes', to quote Janine.

The horse charged on down the road and then, without warning, made a right-hand turn into the scrub. Clunk! Clunk! Then the whole thing came to rest. He'd managed to jam the two shafts neatly between a pair of gum trees. There he stood, poor little fella, puffing, panting and very distressed. There were two people laughing. They were both female, one was Janine and one was my daughter. I wasn't. I was rubbing a rather sore area on my right cheek and I mean the cheek below my waist. There was no sympathy for the driver at all—but the horse got plenty.

That was the beginning and the end of our driving. I felt like Mulga Bill when he spoke of his bicycle saying, 'it's safe at rest ... we'll leave it lying still ... a horse's back is good enough.' Banjo was dead right, you're probably safer on a horse's back than anywhere else. I should report that these days even Janine skirts around all the ads for harness horses. Nevertheless I am becoming just a trifle concerned. There is this rather stunning little Welsh mare that we bred and everyone keeps telling us what a fantastic harness horse she would make. Well, that she may. But if she does, it won't be me taking the first test drive.

Graham Murphy, our saddler, ended up with the harness, the horse and the sulky—and that little cart of ours needed quite a bit of repair work. He campaigned the little fella for a year or two in harness and did exceptionally well. These days

Tony the Pony spends more time with the local kids on his back than he does between the shafts. He's still going strong and all who know him love him. A great little guy.

Real Bushies

20

Lucille

Over the years we have had a couple of wombats and, as animals go, wombats are the greatest. They are halfway between a dog and one of those wind-up toys that races across the floor, bangs into the wall, spins around a few times, and takes off in a totally different direction, all at high speed without any attention to whatever or whoever may be in the way. They also feel a little like warm lead, are solid as rocks, and are physically strong.

The very first wombat we had was a young lady called Lucille. We'd sold the farm at Mole Creek and were living at Moltema at the time. Our good mate Geoff brought her along. It seems her mum had been splattered by a car on one of the local roads and she was sitting there looking fairly dazed and despondent alongside her poor old mum. Mum didn't make it, but Lucille sure did.

To say that wombats are fairly determined creatures is the understatement of the century, and getting Lucille to feed was a major undertaking. She probably weighed just over half a kilo. There have been lots of different formulas to raise orphan animals over the years, but our own particular preference is the Wombaroo brand of product. In those days however formulating the wombat mixture was anything but easy. You mixed the powder with water, stirred the concoction up, added some cream, shook like hell, and then stored the whole frothy mess in an ice-cream tray because you had to make up such large quantities at a time and it wouldn't keep in the ordinary part of the fridge.

Right from the start it was obvious that feeding Lucille was going to be a two-person operation. Janine grabbed hold of the patient while I endeavoured to open the mouth to get the teat in. For those of you who have never raised marsupials, teats come in various shapes and sizes, and the one you use is very much dependent on the type of animal you are going to rear. The majority of teats are fairly long and thin. However, getting this pointed apparatus in the mouth of one very obstreperous wombat was no easy task. I physically prised Lucille's mouth open using half of a dolly clothes peg and then quick as a flash, whipped the teat in. Almost equally as quickly she bit the end off the damn thing, covering all three of us with this gooey, sticky formula. The second attempt netted exactly the same result. Most of the milk went on the outside of the wombat and very little on the inside.

What was needed here was a brains trust capable of out-witting the wombat. For the next few days we fed Lucille with a tube. And I found that if I used an entire wooden clothes peg, pushed into the side of her mouth, I had that small slot in the middle through which I could pass the tube down into her stomach. Now it mightn't have been exactly the way she wanted it, but at least we were getting some tucker into her. Things improved over the next few days, and this very lively youngster began to calm down a bit. Perhaps realising we were intent on helping her rather than trying to choke her, she began at last to take the formula from the teat.

We fed her six times a day to start, always ensuring that her tucker was at the right temperature. In between feeds she was kept warm and cosy inside the sleeve of one of my jumpers. Now wombats are really pretty clean animals; they seem to keep their legs crossed, if you know what I mean, for an incredible length of time. In fact they can go for up to ten hours, and sometimes twelve, without having to visit the necessarium— which does make looking after their toilet habits very easy. Lucille however was to grow up in a household that she shared with a number of cats. At first these poor felines didn't quite know what to make of their new playmate. But as you know, nature is a wonderful thing, and fair dinkum it didn't take long for the wombat and the cats to strike up a bit of a rapport. It got to the stage where she actually enjoyed their heated pet pads (special cat electric blankets) in preference to my tatty old jumper. And she actually learnt to use the litter tray. I kid you not, the funniest thing you have ever seen is a wombat scrabbling around in a litter tray before it evacuates.

Lucille proceeded to grow without a hitch. She weaned herself off the formula and got stuck in to the usual mixture of vegetables, horse food and the inevitable scraps from the table. As time went by she became more adventurous and more entertaining. In fact, she even started to accumulate the odd frequent flyer point. About February some four or five years ago we set off for what was to be the first of many pet expos. We jumped on a plane and headed for Sydney, with Lucille in tow, riding quite happily and totally unfazed in a plastic cat box. The only people who were fazed were the ground staff at the airports en route. Each time Lucille's cage rolled down the luggage conveyer there'd be ten to twenty people pointing and carrying on. But then, just how many people take wombats as unaccompanied luggage?

Getting on the aircraft was no real problem. Down at this

end the staff just take a look and say, 'No worries, it's just Harry's wombat.' But at the other end it becomes a little bit more difficult—especially when you have to smuggle her into a hotel. We developed a pretty ploy for this manoeuvre. I would engage all the staff in avid conversation. Then Janine would drape a large coat over the cage, carry it to the elevator and do a bunk to the floor as quickly as possible.

On one Sydney trip they put us up at a place called the York Mansions, a very impressive building, towards the bottom of Clarence Street, and perched at the very end of the Harbour Bridge. And you wouldn't want to know, they had given us the penthouse. So up we sailed to the top floor. (I should I add here that wombats never give the game away. They don't bark like a dog, or cry like a cat. They just sit there. They are an animal with a lot of patience.) We get out of the lift. Walk in, cases and all, plonk them down and Janine straightaway opens the basket and out of the door flies Lucille. Immediately she is off round and round the apartment, out through the glass doors and onto the balcony! My God, we thought, and charged through the door after her. Not to worry, the balcony did have a pretty solid wall. And standing up on her hind legs, Lucille peaked over the top. I reckon she is the only wombat that has witnessed the peak hour traffic problems on the Harbour Bridge. And we have the pictures to prove it. Whether or not she enjoyed her sojourn at the expo we'll never know; wombats do tend to be very secretive individuals.

By the age of twenty months or so, Lucille was starting to develop some sexual maturity and she became more interested in wandering off than spending time at home with the family. I guess our native animals are a little like our children. You can't own them; they don't belong to us. We have them for a while, I like to think the best part, and then they begin to make their own way in the world. And that is just what Lucille did. We gave her free rein and she would come and go as she pleased. We've moved closer to town now but still on an acreage. There's the river and plenty of nice soft banks covered with thorny blackberries, in which a wombat could feel much more at home. She used to come back occasionally. We would leave some feed outside the back door. But her visits became fewer and finally she came no more. You hope when they go that they are going to be okay. Like I said, Lucille was only loaned to us and we knew one day she would have to go.

21

Our Mate Matilda

It seems that we were never to be without a wombat. I mean, we had all the equipment, the experience and the fantastic fun that Lucille had given us, so when Matilda was plonked in our laps, only a month or two later, we took it all in our stride. Matilda was a lot smaller, she had a lot less hair, she was skinny, she was crook, but she had that gutsy sort of fight and instinct that you knew meant she was going to live. It was a battle for the first few days: antibiotics, fluid therapy, tube feeding, regular maintenance, extra care. But a week down the track, she was feeding from the teat like she had been doing it all her life and growing at a rapid rate. Her skin infection cleared, and her hair started to bristle where there had been only red raw patches and yellow scabs. Her adolescent years were fairly uneventful, but she too soon started on adventures of her own.

One day we were filming in Maitland, just north of Sydney, up in the lovely Hunter Valley, and we had been working all day on a horse property doing stories on Arabian horses and trick riding. Janine had brought Matilda along for the trip—it is difficult to arrange babysitters for wombats; they just don't seem to have the right qualifications, at least not in my wife's eyes. Matilda spent most of the day sleeping quite happily in the little plastic cat box that had been the home for our previous wombat. But when it came time to settle down for the night in the local motel, it was decided that she should have a little more freedom. Now we had been trying to walk her on a lead. But as I recounted previously, wombats are stubborn creatures, and we weren't exactly making stunning progress. It didn't seem to matter what you did, Matilda would select reverse rather than any of the forward gears available in a marsupial's gearbox. And inevitably we'd just stand there looking like prize geese, with a lead and harness hanging limply from our wrists, while the wombat back-pedalled at a million miles an hour. In the end we just gave up.

We had booked into a local motel for the night. It was a family suite, with a small room off to the side for our daughter Heidi. Matilda came out for the usual after-dinner aerobics and proceeded to dash around the floor of the bedroom and lounge room at ever-increasing speed. After all, she had been cooped up all day, and wombats do need to let off a bit of steam occasionally. She didn't seem all that keen on eating, but then she had munched a bit of grass during the day. She took a bottle and we decided that the best place for her would be the bathroom. It had a tiled floor of course, and we thought that with a bit of tucker and her now familiar basket she would be happy in there for the night.

Sometimes when we dream, things seem so real. I was having one of those dreams. And without delving too deeply into my bedroom activities, I can tell you that I tend to sleep on my right side and often dangle my right arm off the side of the bed. I was feeling reasonably comfortable and pretty relaxed given that when you move about as much as I do, you get used to sleeping in lots of different beds. So there I am in the land of nod, hand dangling over the side, and I am dreaming of course, of wombats. I'm also talking to myself, as I frequently do, saying things like, 'Don't do that Matil, cut that out, don't do that.'

Well, I dreamt of her nuzzling my hands, my fingers, and the lower part of my arm. I reckon it took me at least a minute to realise that this wasn't a dream! I flicked on the bedside light, and there's the wombat, scrabbling at the side of the bed, with a sort of 'why don't you pick me up and put me under the covers' look about her. I shook Janine. 'Did you leave the bathroom door open?' I demanded.

'No way,' she said.

'Then how in the hell did the wombat get out?'

'I don't know,' she said.

It was time to get up and investigate. The bathroom door was shut. But, unfortunately, there was a huge hole in the wall. I had heard a few noises, coming from in there before I went to sleep, but quite frankly I didn't think too much of it. Now when I looked inside, I saw that this industrious little wombat of ours had ripped half a dozen tiles off the wall, gone straight through two sheets of gyprock not to mention the insulation, and there she was, smiling and happy, bouncing up and down and demanding to be put into bed with her mother.

It's a little difficult to explain to a motel owner that the hole in the bathroom was in fact caused by a pretty docile looking Australian native animal. But that's the way it is with wombats. They're pretty deceptive. They've often been called the bull-dozers of the bush, and that's a good description. It's a case of charge first and think about it later. Anyway the proprietor was pretty good about the whole thing. The television company paid for the repairs, so he was happy, and he probably renamed the room the Matilda Suite. I must make a note to go back and check it out one day.

Our first house in Relbia, some twenty minutes to the east of Launceston, was built at the very end of a long valley. We looked out on the Esk and the river flats of the neighbouring farm with the lights of Launceston in the distance. It was a pretty spot covering about six hectares. I guess my favourite memory of that place is standing in the kitchen, which looked directly down the valley, and watching our trio of wedgetail eagles ride the wind that funnelled up from the north-west. What sensational birds! Just hanging in midair as if suspended by some non-terrestrial force, sailing, swooping, swerving, and soaring. It's enough to make the hair stand up on the back of your neck. And all this within ten metres of the kitchen window. What a fantastic sight. Anyway, to get back to the story, alongside the kitchen, was a long narrow sunroom. It was beautifully warm, even on a winter's day. We had this brightly coloured green and yellow divan along the back wall. There were ceramic tiles on the floor and the whole thing had a bit of a Mediterranean look about it. Janine's dad loved to sit there when he visited and sort through the many magazines that seemed to accumulate around our home now I was in the television industry.

Wombats have a peculiar way of showing their affection. They normally charge straight at you with their mouths half open. Any of you who have been charged by a wombat will know what I mean. They have four very large front teeth, two on the top and two on the bottom. And they are so pleased to see you that they simply smash into your shins with the greatest possible enjoyment. And that's just what Matilda did to my poor father-in-law while he was seated on the lounge. Bang, straight into the exposed shin bone. There's not a lot of tissue around there, just skin and bone. Damn thing took thirteen weeks to heal. We offered to buy him a pair of cricket pads for future visits.

By the time he had recovered it was time for Matilda and us to move on. We were taking a trip overseas and we had bought a new home, so she and everything else moved while we headed for the United Kingdom. By the time we returned from our trip, Matilda had gone: we had lost another child from our family. Still, as I've said, they know what is best for them. She had a life to lead, just like we all do.

But there is more to this story. It was a cold and very wet Sunday morning, the sort of cold and wet morning we can get in Tassie at any time of the year. The winds blow from the south with all the fury that they can muster as they threaten to transport as much of the Antarctic chill as they can on their journey across the Southern Ocean to our wonderful island.

I was slogging around the place in gumboots when the mobile rang. 'Harry mate,' said David from next door, 'I found a big badger, looks crook, can I bring her around?'

'Sure mate,' I said. 'I'll be home all day.'

'Be round in a flash,' he said.

Now I should interpret this. For those of you who don't know, wombats are known by the locals as badgers. Perhaps it has something to do with the Anglo roots some of us have, but quite honestly, having seen badgers myself, I don't think wombats look much like them at all.

Anyway, David's white ute trundled down the driveway towards our cattery and I met him at the door. Sure enough lying in the back was a big, beautiful, but very sad wombat. She was heavy. We lifted her out and carted her inside. She was cold, she was wet, she was shivering and she couldn't walk. I dried her off with a towel and a hairdryer and had a quick look over her while David looked on. 'She's been lying all night in a ditch, I reckon,' he said. 'And when I rolled her over there in the pouch was a baby about fifteen centimetres long, ice cold, dead.'

I had tears in my eyes. Yeah, I thought, she has been lying all night on her back, with the rain and the sleet belting down on her. Geez I wish people would just stop. It doesn't take a moment to render a bit of help. I mean, cripes, you would do it for anyone else, wouldn't you? Why wouldn't you do it for an animal? And here is my neighbour with twelve hundred acres and a sheep stud, a very successful farmer, and I could see a tear welling up in his eye too. The old girl had the beginnings of pneumonia, severe damage to her spine and pelvis which meant that there was very little feeling and movement in both hind legs. 'We'll give her a go,' I said. 'We can only try.'

So I borrowed an electric heating pad from one of the cats, stuck her on it, ran in some intravenous fluid, antibiotics, and pain killers. Sometimes, it's up to the animal as well. We do what we can, but we can only do so much.

Janine was over in Melbourne at the time at a horse show with George, our black Riding Pony stallion. And we ring each other every night just to keep a check on things. So in the course of conversation that night I happened to tell her the story of the injured wombat. 'I'll be straight home,' she said.

'No need, I reckon.'

'Rubbish,' she said. 'I've finished here anyhow. May as well come home.'

So she did. I picked her up from the airport the next afternoon and by then the sun had managed to fight its way through the clouds and the temperature had in fact climbed to double figures. We went straight down to the cattery so she could check on the progress of my patient. I had kept the poor little baby to show her; it was a girl too. And then of course it was time to look at the patient. She probably looked a little better than she had the previous day; at least she was warm, but she still had virtually no movement in either hind leg, and her breathing was still laboured.

'It's Matilda,' Janine said.

'Don't be so bloody stupid,' I said. 'All wombats look the same.'

'I tell you it's Matilda.'

'You're mad.'

'I'll prove it to you.'

And with that she shot up to the house. A minute or two later she was back with a little parcel of food. 'You watch this,' she said.

And she knelt down in front of the wombat and opened her hand and this wonderful creature seemed almost to gain another hold on life. Her eyes opened, her whiskers twitched and she dragged herself some eighteen inches across the floor to the outstretched hand. She ate. It was the first thing she had eaten in the whole time I'd had her. 'It is her,' she said.

Yes it was. It was Matilda and I felt a mixture of sadness, warmth, happiness and complete incompetence. It was Matilda. How many wombats in the whole of Tasmania eat apricot-flavoured mini-wheats? We cried, we laughed, we remembered—and then we lost her. She died two days later from intractable pneumonia and she is buried in that special place where all our special animals go, on the top of the hill which looks out on our farm, on her home, and the hills through which she wandered. A place where the warm winds blow, a place that is covered by roses of the sweetest perfume and trees that offer shade in the summer and colour in the autumn; a place that is alive with irises and daffodils, our special place.

Matilda came home, and I couldn't save her. But she came home, and that's what matters.

22

Wally Wither Willy

I don't know who creates the more problems in life, girls or boys. You talk to some people, they'll tell you girls are really a headache when they get to their teen years; others will tell you that boys are equally as much a headache at or about the same age. With children, at this stage of the evolutionary pathway, we don't have the ability to choose the sex of our offspring, but with pets, we definitely do.

After all the wombats that have been thrust upon us, the word seemed to get around that the Coopers were somewhat of a dab hand at dealing with orphaned juvenile or adolescent individuals of the species. So guess who arrived one Sunday morning? Yeah, another one, and he was a boy! Things'd been getting out of hand at his first foster home so the poor little bloke got lobbed on us. We called him Wally. Wally with a Willy. That, of course, was to differentiate him from all the females that had gone before.

Now Wally was already fairly well grown when we took him on board. He was off the bottle, eating solid food, and fairly adventurous. We housed him in a large outside run with an earthen floor and he proceeded to dig himself a burrow in a corner and let himself in and out whenever he liked. Now Wally's comings and goings didn't worry us too much. He was a pretty independent sort of a sod, but funnily enough he was extremely affectionate. Wally also joined the frequent flyer club when we shipped him up to Nambour in Queensland for the local garden festival. Queensland is pretty short on wombats. They've got a few of the hairy-nosed variety right down in the south-east corner and they're highly endangered, but not much else. So Wally was going to be something of a sensation.

The local press were there to meet us. We had to fly independently, because I'd been busy elsewhere and Janine had carted Wally up from home with the usual amount of excitement that travelling wombats seem to engender. A journalist from the local paper was there to get a story on our illustrious wombat and a photographer was on hand to snap a few pretty pictures as well. So while I was waiting for Janine and Wally to arrive, we got the interview over and done with.

Now I like to interview people who are interviewing me, because I figure if they want to know all there is to know about me, I reckon I need to know a little bit about them. And it turns out that this young lady of the press had not long landed on our shores from the country of the maple leaf and the moose. Those of you who know me, or have heard me, know that I have very little respect for the Queen's English, to the degree that if my poor mother were alive today she would still be remonstrating with me about my poor pronunciation and the use of so many Aussie-isms. After five minutes it was pretty obvious to me there was something of a language barrier. That proved to be true, for there, next morning on the front page of the paper, under a glorious picture of all three of us, with Wally in centre stage, displaying all his masculine glory was the caption 'WALLY WITHER WILLY VISITS NAMBOUR'. Yeah, like I said, a real language barrier.

Nonetheless he was the hit of the show. Loved people.

And was totally unfazed by all the attention paid to him.

Back at home, Wally settled into his lifestyle just as if nothing had happened. His comings and goings seemed to be more frequent and quite frankly we often wondered just where he went on his nocturnal expeditions. Now wombats are just that, nocturnal, and most of the day they're holed up in their burrows. But come nightfall they're out and about feeding and doing what I suppose most adult wombats, or adults of any description, like to do.

It was Tasmania. It was July. It was two o'clock in the morning. The phone rang. Janine can never work out why it is that regardless of what time the phone rings during the night, I can be instantly awake and, not only that, fully aware of what is going on. When you've been a vet on duty for as long as I have it, just comes naturally. This call was from our neighbour. Well our old neighbour. And the conversation went something like this.

'It's about your wombat.'

'Yeah,' I said, 'what about the wombat?'

'It ... it ... it ... it ... it's ... it's in the pool.' Our neighbour was inclined to stutter when he got excited. Couple all that with a Pommie accent he never really lost and he was more than a little difficult to understand.

'In the pool,' I said.

'Y ... Y ... Y ... Y ... Y ... Yes,' he stammered.

'Well 'elp it out,' I said.

'I ... I ... I ... I ... I can't catch it.'

Strike me lucky, I thought. 'All right, I'll be there in a minute.'

It was fair dinkum freezing, Jack Frost had been working overtime. I had on a nightshirt and not much else. So I pulled on a heavy dressing gown, pair of slippers, stumbled into the car and drove next door, well actually it was on the opposite side of the laneway we shared.

The joint was lit up like a Christmas tree. Every light must have been on. I knew where the pool was, headed straight for it. Pointed the lights of the car in the general direction, and there he was, my neighbour, rugged up to the hilt, standing there like some field marshal, commanding the troops on the beach at the D-Day landings. The only thing missing was the baton under his arm. And, sure enough, there's Wally, streaking up and down the pool like a regular Michael Klim. Heaven knows what record he was after. Now I don't know what kind of stroke wombats do. In fact, I didn't know they could swim at all. They're that damn heavy I thought they'd sink like a rock. Anyway, I leant over and tried to grab him. No way mate. Wally was having none of that. All the while our neighbour kept muttering obscenities under his breath and I couldn't get near the little monster. Every time I lunged for him, he swerved out of the way. It was obvious what was going to happen. I was going to get wet! Stripped down to my undies and jumped in. No idiot goes swimming at two o'clock in the morning in July, and certainly not in Tasmania, and definitely not in an unheated pool. It was bloody freezing!

Wally was so happy to see me. 'Dad,' he must have said, 'glad you could join me.'

And he sprinted over to show his affection in the only way he could, clawing several deep furrows in my frozen torso as I grappled for a hold on the nuggetty little fella. He was as lively as a cricket as the pair of us struggled back to the steps. Wally thought the whole experience was wonderful and seemed ecstatic that I should have joined him in his aquatic

adventures. I got out of the pool, still wrestling with Wally, shivering, standing there, dripping wet, and dying to get home, but now the field marshal was going to give me a lecture.

I wasn't in the mood for any dissertation I can tell you. I slung Wally in the tray of the station wagon, wrapped the dressing gown around me and confronted the neighbour.

'Your wombat is a real problem.'

'Oh yeah,' I said, 'what's he done now?'

'He ... He ... He ... He's terrified the dog.'

I found out later what was actually happening. Wally was a smart little sod. He worked out that this little Jack Russell of theirs got fed every night on the front verandah. He'd hide in the bushes and as soon as the food was down, and those humans were out of the way, Wally would just muscle in and take over. The poor wretched dog would fly around to the back door in panic, furiously scratch on it, demanding to be let in. Wally was up to that one too. As soon as he had finished the tucker, he would streak around to the back door and start scratching too. All of this would add further insecurity to the Jack Russell's general lack of emotional well-being. He'd start crying in absolute terror and disappear upstairs to hide under the bed.

'The ... the ... the ... there's more,' the neighbour went on.

Strike, by now I really am cold. 'What then?' I snapped.

'I ... I ... I ... It's the house,' he said.

Turned out poor ol' Wally had built himself a little holiday home. Yep. Carved out a magnificent burrow under the south-east corner of the house, right under the main bedroom. It had caused the foundations to subside and they had to employ some underpinners to straighten the whole thing up. But the last straw, apart from the pool episode of course, had happened just the night before.

Wally had been intent on doing some gardening at the same time as our neighbour was having a conference call with his family in England. Now nothing gets in the way of a wombat intent on his horticultural pursuits. That of course, includes phone cables! You've guessed it. Right in the middle of the call, lights out, Wally goes straight through the cable. Surely there couldn't be anymore. And thank God there wasn't. Wally and I went home. I had a hot shower, he went into solitary and next morning we devised a battle plan to deal with Wally.

Transportation was the only answer. Wally's moved up country now. He still comes to the back door, they tell me, three or four times a week for his special treats. But he must have a few lady friends by now because his visits are becoming less frequent as time goes by. Who knows, he may very well be assembling his very own swim team for the next wombat olympics. Good on ya, Wal.

23

Harriet

Our last wombat was a young lady called Harriet. Now you don't normally go shopping for wombats. But in a roundabout sort of a way, that's exactly what happened. There was Janine pushing the trolley around the local supermarket, trying to get more for less, but as usual getting less for more. And who should pass by but a fellow shopper with a little bundle of rags propped up in her trolley. My wife will never die without knowing. I sometimes think she is a bit of a sticky beak actually. So of course she had to have a look inside this bundle. And guess what? There's a wombat.

Now I caught up with this wombat some few hours later and I could tell you it was a pretty miserable looking specimen. Diarrhoea, dehydration and what an old colleague of mine would describe as a 'severe degree of crookness'. There's no way Janine was going to leave this wombat to breathe its last in a supermarket trolley. It wasn't being fed the correct diet and would surely have expired had things continued. 'You'd better give it to me,' she said. 'I'll fix it.'

And sure enough we did.

Harriet was the smallest we had ever taken on board. But she fed well. And it only took a couple of days on good old Wombaroo and she was full steam ahead. A bit of the old Protexin—sort of like a yoghurt for animals—full of all the right sort of good bacteria to establish a normal population in the bowels. Great stuff. She was probably more cat-like than dog-like. And very much a lady. Probably a little quieter than our previous lot. But nonetheless as entertaining as any of them. Her only problem was she liked to dig. Now when you have lino, digging can be a problem—even worse on carpet. And Harriet hated being alone. I've got three doors to prove that. Talk about carve your initials, I reckon she has written her full name three times. So it was down to the stables for her. Concrete floor, solid walls, and that's where she stayed. Until, it was time for us to go on holidays.

It takes a very special person to babysit a wombat. By now, Harriet was well over twelve months old, very independent, but would happily follow you around the farm like a dog at heel. Having said that, we always kept our wombats well away from the dogs. I believe it is essential for them to have a natural fear of dogs. It will certainly save them in any emergency. So where to put Harriet, that was the question. Now believe it or not I do have a few pretty good mates. In fact both of us do. And after consultation, not with Harriet, but with our mate, it was decided she should spend her vacation at Mole Creek.

Androo Kelly runs Trowana Wildlife Park. And wombats are second nature to him. Over the years I've got pretty involved with him, helped as much as I can with his Tassie Devil project, and rendered veterinary assistance whenever I could. He was happy to take Harriet. So with all pomp and ceremony out we went and plonked her in a run with another wombat of about the same age. She wasn't very big; I think that her growth may have been partly affected by her early child-hood problems. The other wombat sidled over with a sort of 'glad to see you' attitude, but no way was Harriet having any of that. She was no wombat. She'd been living with humans.

She didn't recognise wombats, she just recognised people. And as visitors came strolling down the path she was more intent on making friends with them than with any other marsupial in the vicinity. We were off the next day, I knew she would be okay. Androo would put her through the same desensitising process that he used on all his wombats. This simply means that they are exposed less and less to people and more and more to their own kind.

Janine couldn't wait to get back to find out how she was. We even sent her a postcard from Ireland! And I think Androo had his hands full. She only stayed in the run for one day and then proceeded to climb in and out just as she pleased, still more intent on following people around the park than on anything else. That lasted for about a fortnight and then she went feral. She dug a huge burrow, right under Androo's koala exhibit and no manner of coaxing from us could get her out for a quick reunion. These days he tells me she's the boss of the place—digs in and out, climbs over fences, burrows where she pleases. She bobs up where you least expect her and is about as unpredictable as any wombat could be.

She hasn't grown a lot more but the word is that she is looking a little larger towards the rear end than she did before. And Androo is pretty certain there's a little Harriet—or could it be a Harry—growing in that pouch. If we can ever coax her out of the burrow perhaps we'll all find out.

24

Alternative Lifestyle

Wombats in veterinary practice present problems that are very peculiar to the breed. We have all the usual routine stuff, like overgrown nails, mange, and dental problems, not to mention other assorted skin diseases and the usual run of tummy upsets. In the main though, they're as tough as teak. I guess because we'd reared a few by now, I seemed to attract quite a few wombats with problems. I had a pretty regular influx of patients from an area just outside Deloraine. It was a neck of the woods where a lot of people lived what I guess you would describe as a pretty relaxed—or shall we say different—lifestyle.

Now one of these clients who seemed to funnel all these wombats my way, lived with her partner in a house that really was wombat friendly. In fact their place was specially designed to cater for the every foible of these wonderful animals. They did tell me that at one stage there were thirty-five of them living in and around the home. The mind boggles, doesn't it. Where there were doors in the house they were hinged with those old-fashioned sort of hinges that were spring loaded, allowing the doors to swing in either direction and come back to a central position. Not only that, they had taken care to screw some galvanised iron to both sides of the door up to a height of about two feet from the floor. The wombats would fair dinkum charge these doors, fling 'em open and manage to slip through before they closed again. They had it down to a fine art. This was made all the easier by the fact that I think that wombats have got the neatest bum of any animal I have ever met. Out of interest, they are the koala's closest relation, and have the same hard bony plate on top of their pelvis which they use to great effect when they're defending their burrow. They simply jam their backside in the entrance and, believe you me, nothing gets past a wombat's backside. From a design point of view, and when viewed from the side, I guess it has what I would call a very neat and aerodynamic rear end. A wombat's tail, and it does have one, is tiny. Very thin and probably only three-quarters of an inch long. They tuck it right in when they are on the move and this compact posterior makes it impossible for anything at all to get caught in the door.

It was a Thursday when this woman came in with a large, aged female wombat wrapped in a couple of towels and cradled in her arms. I'd seen the patient before. She'd had a dental problem. Wombats' front teeth sometimes grow a little askew and need to be trimmed back. I found the best tool was an angle grinder. Sounds horrific, I know, but bear in mind, we are dealing with damn strong teeth and a damn strong animal. They don't split and they don't leave any sharp edges. The only problem is holding the wombat still. Anyway this wasn't the problem today. She really was sick—breathing heavily, and I could hear fluid bubbling around inside those lungs of hers. Early pneumonia and pleurisy was my diagnosis. Her temperature was normal and she was still eating, so the prognosis was reasonable. Antibiotics and some good old TLC were prescribed and I knew my instructions would be carried out to the letter.

Come Saturday morning she was back for a revisit and

looked shocking. By this time her temperature had dropped to one degree below normal, both lungs were severely congested, she'd stopped eating and had three feet on the grave and another one on a banana skin. The look on my face must have been enough. My client started to cry. I'm a pretty touchy-feely sort of a person and I guess I just reached out and put my arm around her and said 'Come on, it's just a wombat.'

She pulled away, spun around and through the tears cried, 'It's more than just a wombat.'

She was right. In all my thirty years that was the stupidest thing I have ever said. It's only just a wombat. No way. This was a child, her child, more than just a wombat. Geez, I wished the floor had opened up and swallowed me. She stood there cradling her baby with tears flowing down her face and her simple cotton dress splattered with mud and dirt from the animal she held in her arms. If I didn't pull this wombat through, after what I'd said, I don't reckon I could have lived with myself.

When you go through life I find you build up a sort of bank balance of favours, things you do for people that one day they may be able to repay in some way, shape or form. This was the time to call in a few favours. Launceston General Hospital was probably the place to go. There are many potent antibiotics used in human medicine that we as vets don't stock in our arsenal. Frankly they are just too expensive and we would use them so infrequently they would probably go out of date before they're needed. I knew what I needed, and they had it. The only problem was, how to get it from Launceston to Exton some thirty minutes away before everything shut down at lunchtime on Saturday, as places have a habit of doing on this little island.

With her bare feet and her unkempt hair my client looked a pretty miserable sight. But I knew her partner had a job that really might come in handy. He was a chauffeur for one of the local parliamentary ministers—and he had a mobile phone! A quick call and the government car was picking up the necessary from the hospital and on its way out to the surgery. You could imagine the reaction from the clients in the waiting room when the government car pulls up, flag fluttering, at the front door of the clinic, and in strides the uniformed driver, parcel in hand.

My client had had a lot of nursing experience and she was used to giving injections and all the physiotherapy that I had prescribed for our wombat. Treatment four times daily, fluids by mouth and warmth were paramount if we were going to pull the old girl through. I've got to be honest, I wasn't that optimistic. It was a holiday weekend, so it was Tuesday before I was likely to hear much of what was to happen.

At about eleven o'clock up they rocked. In the old bomb Volkswagen, still in bare feet, and possibly the same dress, it was hard to tell, she carried the old girl through the door. She was smiling and I was smiling and you know I think the wombat was smiling too. Temperature normal. Lungs clearing and she was beginning to eat on her own. She was over the hill and well on her way to recovery. We needed to keep the therapy going for at least another week to make sure there was no relapse, but one thing had puzzled me, so I asked the question.

'How did you manage to keep her warm?'

You see I knew they had no electricity and no running water except for stuff in the creek, fifty metres or so from the back door.

'Well,' she said, 'it's like this. I went home, took off all my

185

clothes, got into bed with the wombat and I only got out to go to the toilet.'

That's right, she'd spent the whole three days in bed cuddling the wombat to her own body to keep it warm. She was right. I was wrong. It was more, much more, than just a wombat.

Talking With
the Animals

25

Elephant Talk

They say elephants never forget, and for me, my close encounter with elephants is something I won't forget in a hurry either. Perth Zoo was home to three young Asian elephants. Things were pretty crook back where they came from. Somewhere up the Malay Peninsula land clearing for farming was on the increase, and elephants were being pushed more and more into an ever-decreasing jungle habitat. The farmers found them hard to deal with because at night these lovable grey giants would leave the shelter of the jungle to raid the crops. It was easy pickings for them, all those lush beautiful vegetables, not to mention the sugarcane. Some of the landholders had taken things into their own hands, and consequently the very survival of the species was in jeopardy.

To ensure the preservation of these huge mammals, Perth Zoo had taken on board three young orphans, two females and one male. Similar ventures were to happen at zoos and wildlife parks all over the globe. With so many endangered species, captive breeding programs are the only way that many can be preserved and Australia is doing its part with quite a number of animals from different parts of the world, the black rhino breeding complex at Western Plains Zoo in Dubbo being a prime example. Animals are endangered these days for so many different reasons, and in the majority of cases humans are either directly or indirectly responsible. The rhinoceros, valued for its horn, is slaughtered to this day by poachers intent on making a fast buck. And for what? Supposed medical properties of the horn. What properties? Horns are nothing more than hair! Hair that is compressed together so tightly that it assumes the strength of bone, but hair nonetheless.

Through agricultural pursuits that involve the decimation of forests and loss of habitat, the urban sprawl, and the pollution of so many rivers and lakes by industrial effluent, every day some species teeters on the brink of extinction. We truly are a ruthless race. It seems to me we were given 'dominion' over the animals if we are to believe the biblical account. But to have dominion over something is to have a ruler's control, and with it goes the responsibility to govern properly. My friends, we abdicated that responsibility many years ago. But enough of my preaching, time to get back to those babies I was talking about.

They were only little critters—well little as elephants go— but all three stood taller than me and weighed a lot more as well. At first glance they looked a little lost, after all they'd not been here all that long. But the three formed a close-knit group and yet, in spite of their obvious size advantage, seemed to have quite a deal of respect for their keepers and any other human that ventured into their enclosure. I wondered just what memories they had of contact with the human race. It was the human race that had made them orphans!

There's a lot involved in looking after an elephant. The day begins with a bath—and not just a quick go-over with the hose, but a full-on scrub down for almost an hour. It's pretty tiring work, playing the hose over their back, down the sides and then scrubbing away with the brush to shift any scurfy material off the skin. It's an essential part of their daily care because it stim-ulates blood flow and ensures a healthy epidermis—and a pachyderm without a good epidermis is a pretty uncomfortable one. What's more, they love it. They're almost smiling and laughing as you scrub away, starting at the very top of their head, making your way down the neck, the back, the belly and all four legs. Even the feet get a good go-over. All the time the trunk is swaying rhythmically backwards and forwards, while at the other end what must be the most pathetic excuse for a tail keeps time with the general mood of things.

Young elephants learn from older elephants. The zoo had an aged elephant, totally unrelated to these guys. She was well over thirty and became their matriarch, teacher, and adopted aunty. And if you thought the babies were small, she was enormous. There were lots more things to do. For a start she had to be washed as well. Then the whole group had to be exercised, which meant a walk around the zoo before the doors were open to the public. Baby elephants are pretty inquisitive and that trunk of theirs can get up to plenty of trouble, believe you me. They really were just like three naughty kids, pulling at this and that and I reckon, given half the chance, they'd have got up to all sorts of mischief. Finally, back at their daytime enclosure it was time for a dust bath. So, just like any kid, having been scrubbed from head to toe and made as clean as any vet could make them, they immediately proceeded to get filthy dirty again. Dust and dirt and finally mud and slurry flew in all directions. I think they were far happier when they were dirty. After all, the mud and dirt was there for a definite purpose, for in the wild there was no way you could pop down to the local elephant pharmacy and pick up half a gallon or so of sunblock. The mud dried on the skin and did the job instead.

Lunch soon followed, a delicious concoction of fruit and vegetables, sugarcane, bamboo, and rough branches. The way in which they use that trunk of theirs to eat is quite incredible. The tip has an almost finger-like projection which they use to pick up tiny little morsels, like peanuts and almonds. The dexterity would amaze you.

It was late in the afternoon and time to head in another direction. We'd been filming all day, at other sites around the zoo, and the final sequence was not too far away. The producer wanted a really nice kissy, cuddly sort of shot to finish the show. First of all we laid out a line of food, their favourites of chopped carrots and apples, and then with the help of the keepers we organised the three little guys in a row, behind the food, all looking at the camera—well, when they weren't eating anyhow. I took up a spot in the middle between two of the babies while in the background, right behind me, was good ol' aunty. We took a few shots, I spelled out my usual closing lines, and really felt a little sorry that the day had come to a close. It had been a real privilege working with these little orphans and their foster mum.

Then as we went for one final take, a wonderful thing happened. One of those things that you don't expect but when it arrives you'd wish it would never end. From out of nowhere this huge trunk appeared before my eyes, it turned and looked squarely into my face, and then began to explore the whole of my facial anatomy with its very wet and sticky end. All over the cap, the forehead, the cheeks, the lips, my glasses—now all askew and totally blurred—and then inside my shirt and the singlet and God knows where else. Then out of nowhere a little tiny squeak. A pause for a moment, then another tiny little squeak, a mouse-like little squeak.

'Who said that?' I asked the keeper.

'It's the old girl,' he said. How, I thought, could a massive animal weighing tons possibly emit a squeak so small. Then she said it again, and again, and I turned around to look.

There behind me was this huge, grey, ponderous, wild animal, with the smallest of deep brown eyes, gargantuan flapping ears, a skin like coarse sandpaper and the wettest of noses. A slow, powerful, but lovable creature, still intent on exploring every part of my being. Not with her eyes, but with her trunk.

'Why,' I asked, 'did she make a noise like that?'

'Oh,' he said, 'they do that when they're happy.'

Well, poor ol' dumb me had to ask, 'Why is she happy?'

'You know,' he said, 'she really likes you.'

An elephant likes me. Really likes me. A tear in my eye said it all. To get so close to such a massive creature, to be trusted is something, but to be liked is just the best.

26

Way Up North

Ranua Zoo in Finland used to be the northernmost zoo in the world until another one was built a bit closer to the North Pole a few years back. We flew from Helsinki, the capital of this country they call 'the land of a thousand lakes', to Rovaniemi almost slapbang on the Arctic Circle. About a two-hour trip. It was towards the end of the northern summer so the days were long and the nights were bright—and the mosquitoes were enormous, probably the biggest I've ever seen. The place was renowned for them. Thank heavens we'd missed the worst of the onslaught.

There were lots of things to do. Santa's workshop was close by and you could enjoy Christmas all year round, relive your childhood and see the smiles on the faces of the visiting children as they spoke in all kinds of languages to the whiskery old gentleman who seemed to understand what they were saying. Incidentally, I did speak personally to Santa later and he informed me that he could converse in seven languages. How pathetic do you think I felt? I can't even speak English properly. Well, so my dear mother often used to tell me.

Nearby are reindeer farms and what a wonderful animal reindeers really are, providing transportation, clothing and food for the people of the Arctic North. Quietly and almost regally they wander backwards and forwards across water-soaked pastures to be called by their herders dressed in the vivid blues and reds of the typical Lapp costume. These farms are only small, mostly around thirty acres, and the paddocks even smaller, some not much bigger than a suburban building block. Farming these gentle animals is perhaps a lesson in management for many of our so-called modern farming enterprises. They are penned during the short weeks when the succulent summer grasses grow freely throughout the countryside, and in the winter months simply turned out to wander where they will and scavenge for food amidst the tundra. These deer, with their perhaps legendary status, search for their own special food, a fungus which they can sniff out beneath half a metre or more of snow. Some may browse branches from the many deciduous trees, which grow abundantly in the forested regions. They manage in spite of the cold and adversity to not only survive but prosper. Some industrious farmers even make hay by hand, cuttting the long lanky water grasses with a scythe, then carrying the fodder in huge bundles up to racks to dry in the summer sun. The paddocks are crisscrossed by long tent-like structures on which this rather different hay is drying. And, unlike during our summers, there's not as much heat around so the process can take quite a few weeks.

But I'd come to see the zoo, Ranua Zoo. The director was a vet, so we had lots in common and lots to talk about. She was without doubt the most exuberant colleague I had ever met, and spoke with such enthusiasm about her charges that the whole visit was bound to be exciting. The first thing that strikes you about the place is that it's quiet, incredibly quiet. There is no background noise. No trucks, cars, or buses, nothing like the constant rumble that pervades most of our daily lives. Absolute peace. We were a long long way from anywhere. There weren't a lot of people there either; the main tourist season was over and only a few stragglers were bothering to come and pay a visit.

'It's the zoo where your feet never touch the ground,' I was told.

And how true that was. Not in the supernatural sense, but for real! The tundra is a unique area. It's fragile, it's beautiful, it's irreplaceable. The tramp of human progress damages it irreparably. At Ranua they've managed the whole thing magnificently, for everywhere you go there are boardwalks, suspended some half a metre or so above the intricate vegetation which, when I was there, was starting to assume some of its stunning autumn colour. Lichens, mosses and ground-hugging perennials provided a mish-mash of shapes and colours that only a visit to the place could accurately describe. It is an area I dearly love to visit. It seems almost primitive. Between the belts of forest with its deep green conifers and yellowing birches and larches, the open country is a mass of greens, purples, oranges, reds and yellows—an autumn display that you never get to see in our part of the world.

The zoo specialised in exhibiting animals that were found almost exclusively in the vast Arctic areas of the world, and first up were the otters. The director had reared three of these in her own home and reckoned they were the most mischievous creatures the good Lord had ever put breath in. They loved it when she walked into their enclosure. Being wonderful, playful animals the otters ducked and darted around her legs and over her feet as she shuffled her way from one end to the other, like a bunch of hyperactive and very wet puppies. Talk about energy, there was no stopping these guys. Boy did they get up to some pranks. There were lots of stories of losing them for a day and suddenly finding them all asleep in the linen press. Or she would be relaxing in the bath, only to have her mood broken by these three slippery individuals who really prefer water to dry land anytime. They even managed to get inside the fridge. You'd open a door and there would be an otter. You'd pull back the bedspread, and there'd be an otter, just having a little nap under the blankets. You couldn't keep track of these playful little devils for anything longer than a minute. Trying to hold onto one was damn near impossible, they were so slippery, and seemed able to turn themselves completely inside-out within their own body length. On top of all that they seemed to spend the whole time laughing at you as if the whole episode—and even life itself—was one big joke.

Birds have always been favourites of mine and there was a magnificent collection of owls, in particular, the Snowy Owls. These beautiful birds with their stunning frosty feathers are perfectly camouflaged in the winter landscape. They have huge rounded eyes with those typical circular facial features, and they sit almost motionless on their perches. Owls, you know, have very special feathers. The main flight feathers on their wings are modified in such a way that the edges are ever so slightly frayed. When the birds fly they do it almost noiselessly—a pretty handy trick when you're out hunting at night. Their ears too are arranged in such a way that they can track the sounds of their quarry with incredible accuracy, very much like underwater sonar is used to track submarines.

I got a chance to see some unusual animals as well, like lemmings, tiny little rodent-like creatures who apparently commit suicide every so often by charging into the sea. I saw pine martins, minks, pole cats, stoats and weasels—all ferret-like animals, totally unknown in our neck of the woods. A large herd of reindeer, a magnificent group of bear, moose and other breeds made the collection quite stunning. The camera was working overtime. It's not every day you get to see such a diverse group of animals from the other side of the world.

I can remember illustrations of an horrific creature called a wolverine from comics as a child, and memories of these stories seemed to paint the animal as some huge, bear-like creature. Nothing could be further from the truth. They aren't that big. They're probably not even as big as a fox. However, they don't look very pretty, and two or three of them are capable of killing an adult reindeer without any effort at all—and not just one or two of these gentle animals, but a whole herd, if the wolverines are in the mood. These guys are thrill killers. They do it because they love to do it. Sure they have to eat, but they really enjoy the kill more. And there I was, sitting in the enclosure calling 'em over to feed from my fingertips. Yeah, sometimes I reckon I am crazy. Thank God, my insurance agent wasn't on hand.

The wolverines were shy, but interested in what I held in my hand nonetheless, and in time they got closer and closer to the offering. When they walked, the whole front foot, from the toes right up to the back of their wrist, was flattened on the ground, unlike a cat or a dog that simply walks on its toes. In a way it was like a huge snowshoe, a special modification that allowed them to get around in the winter, when the snow was soft and fresh. Their back feet were much the same. Coat colours were a mixture of black and brown, with tiny little ears, a broad skull, short but pointed face, and a long bushy tail. They didn't smell all that charming however, and a quick brush through their matted hair wouldn't have gone astray. All in all they had a pretty mean look about them. Quick as a flash one would dart in, grab a bit of food, dart out again. Boy those teeth were mean and you could hear the molars crunching on the chicken bones that they'd grabbed from my fingers. Y'know in time most animals will come around. It's the curiosity factor I think—plus the fact that there I was at their level, sitting on the ground, not really posing a threat. And of course I had the ultimate in bribery—food. After almost an hour with these guys, I actually had them sniffing around the old RM Williams boots. But you can only push things just so far, so I retreated gracefully before they fancied a feed on those as well.

You always leave the best till last, they say, and I'm so pleased we did. She was a cat. A lynx. A big cat. I reckon around thirty-five pounds all up (or say sixteen kilos in the metric language). And all muscle. She'd been hand-reared by my host and had no fear of humans whatsoever. As you walked past the front of her enclosure she stalked you all the way along, hiding in the undergrowth, and then jumping out in mock attack at your feet as you passed. I love big cats and went back for a second look.

'Would you like to go in?' the director asked.

Would I what! In we went.

'Now whatever you do,' she said, 'don't bend down.'

'Why on earth not?'

'She'll jump on you.'

Stand back, I thought, this is going to be a great experience.

I walked halfway down the track that this big, beautiful, furry, pussy cat had worn between the foliage. That put me some fifteen metres from the front of the cage. I could half see her out of the corner of my eye, crouching low and watching my every movement. I was the prey and she was the hunter.

There is just something super terrific about a big cat. They are a beautiful sight. A soft, brindle-brownish colour, lighter underneath with spots up and down the legs, longer hair around their face and neck and black tufts sticking out from the tops of their ears. Their eyes are outlined with black mascara and white eyeshadow. What a sensational animal. I picked my spot and squatted close to the ground. Nothing happened. I waited, nothing happened. Five minutes passed, still nothing and then my poor old knees started to ache. I relaxed and lowered my posterior onto the soft earth. She sprang! From where I've no idea, and landed fair on my shoulders. Big sharp claws dug in and held on. I only had a shirt on my back. Thirty-five pounds of feline fur and claws scraping through a pretty flimsy bit of clothing for a better grip immediately drew a drop of blood, and a gasp as well.

'You all right?' asked the director.

'I'll be right. Don't worry.'

You see this was something very special and, pain or not, I was going to enjoy every minute of the experience. She played with me like I was a toy. Thumping me here and thumping me there with her front feet, never with malice just like a game of shadow-boxing. Then up again onto my shoulders, around my head, off went the cap and she started to chew on my poor bald head. With her big front paw over each ear I didn't have much chance of getting away and she started to lick and growl as she mouthed the whole of my skull. Sure there were plenty of fairly deep scratches, but then vets get plenty of those in practice every week so a few more wouldn't even be noticed. The chance to relate so closely to an animal that really is still wild is for me the greatest experience in the world. Big cats are so beautiful and, my furry lady friend, I won't ever forget our time together.

The whole episode lasted around ten minutes. Sure, I was okay And she was okay too. There was a bit of blood about— but so what? It was all in good fun and I was just beginning to enjoy it when she leapt away and took off into the shrubbery. Standing up and walking back to the door I could see her still, just hoping I'd do something else to excite her, and just out of reach. As I made for the exit, she made for my legs. You could sidestep for all you're worth, but it was a perfect rugby tackle and down I came again. I don't fall too elegantly either, particularly when I'm being tackled by a four-legged feline. She went straight for my head again and off came the cap. That wasn't what interested her, there seemed to be something about that noggin of mine, because that's just what she went for all over again.

When I finally got out, a little bit out of shape and a little bit bloodier than normal, everyone else seemed more concerned than me. I'd loved it. What the hell were they worried about? And what was the attraction about that head of mine? Well, it turns out I'd been stupid enough to smother the whole of my scone with mosquito repellent and, as my colleague proceeded to tell me at some length, 'she really gets high on that stuff'!

So just how do you top a day like that? The answer is I don't think you can. My wife and I often sit and look at the camera footage of that afternoon. Janine is still one very jealous lady and you can bet on one thing if ever we get back to Ranua it will take a superhuman effort to keep her out of the Lynx enclosure, for even though she's experienced the Dream World tigers in Surfers Paradise in a very close encounter, nothing equates to being stalked by a Lynx.

27

Big Cats

Television has been good to me. 'Talk to the Animals' was a wonderful program that took me all over the world. I've been to America, England and Asia, but for sheer animal indulgence there is nothing that can equal Africa. No television screen, no picture postcard, no cinema can convey the magnitude of Africa's animal scene. There are not thousands, there are not hundreds of thousands, there are millions of animals inhabiting a landscape so large that it can be hard for the human mind to encompass. The country seems to stretch into eternity. You feel almost drunk with the intensity and the enormity of the scenes that confront you.

We toured around Kenya and the great Serengeti Plain, the flat expanse of the Masai Mara, punctuated only by the odd low hill and dry river bed. We witnessed the migration of the wildebeest towards the Mara River. What force drives these animals is unknown, but they wander in their millions, heads down, never looking further than a metre or two in front, heading always slowly onwards towards a river crossing that must see the death of one in every ten of them. There are not just wildebeest making this annual trek. There are antelope and zebra, giraffe and warthogs, and of course the predators. Lions, leopards and cheetah follow, for where the grass-eaters go, so do they. All the animals seem remarkably tolerant of the khaki-clad tourists who spend their days travelling around

mainly in little vans with pop-up lids on top. These vehicles are treated I guess, as part of the landscape and pose no threat. We were in one of those.

The guides invariably know where all the action is, and the bush telegraph is very active. One afternoon, we'd heard there were a couple of cheetah camped on the side of a hill looking down on a herd of wildebeest in a dry creek bed below. When we arrived there were already half a dozen or so vans parked in an inverted L-configuration to the side and above the cheetah. We pulled in above them, alongside another bunch of tourists. The cheetah were no more than twenty-five metres in front of us. Boy, what a sight. The grass was dry and long and while ever they remained lying they were impossible to detect. Every so often one would sit bolt upright just the way cheetah do, on their haunches, those long thin front legs stretched taut and straight, just like those ceramic statues from some fancy art deco shop. With their small heads and ears, and the black tear marking streaming from the corner of each eye, they are built for one thing only—and that is speed.

Below them some fifty metres or more away moved the wildebeest. In a long dusty line they inched their way along the dusty depression, wending in and out between the thorny acacias. I reckon three hundred was probably fairly close to the mark, and half of them had already passed by the time we arrived. The cheetah took turns sitting up and staring at these ungainly animals. They were waiting, patiently waiting. Alongside me the camera was rolling, homing in on these regal hunters, and their prey, in the shallow valley below.

Now Noel the cameraman had had a problem once before with cats and we'd never, ever let him forget it. Singapore Zoo was the venue. The fishing cat the subject. There sat the cat on the side of the pond, immobile, rigid, as if glued to the spot, staring hypnotically into the water watching the goldfish swim lazily past. Noel filmed and filmed until finally after twenty-nine minutes and almost the end of the tape, he buttoned off. The very moment he did, the cat jumped in.

Such a thing was never going to happen again to Noel, so he just kept rolling on these two cheetah. Finally the tape ran out. He sat down with a sort of 'I give up' look on his face. But yours truly was having a sensational time. My camera equipment wasn't all that schmick but I'd learnt a few tips from wildlife photographer, Jonathon Scott, with whom we'd spent a day earlier in the trip. He'd even given me one of his sandbags on which to rest the camera and lens. There I was, perched up on a chair, head out of the pop-top, camera, a 300mm telephoto, and a doubler all screwed into place—600mm of photographic fun. It was sensational. Every time one of them stood up, I hit the cable release, they filled the frame, fantastic. I reckon it was at least another ten minutes or so before one cheetah finally stood right up, on all four legs. What a sight. The auto wind was working overtime, as frame after frame flashed through the lens. He stared intently at the last of the wildebeest shuffling slowly behind the herd—the old, the infirm, the young and the injured. Like a military general he surveyed the arena. Then he turned to look at the audience. Slowly at first he swung his gaze away from the wildebeest, and then up the hill, in a slow arc he moved his stare from one van to another. Finally he stopped at me.

Have you ever been eyeballed by a big cat? Boy, it's something. I could feel the hair stand up on the back of my neck. My hands sweated just a little. I seemed for a moment unable to press the damn cable release. It would have been a good thirty seconds that we stood there with no more than twenty-five metres of dry grass between us. Click ... shlunk ... click ... shlunk, at last the camera came to life, as my thumb steadied on the release button. He never moved. He never blinked. He just stared, those massive eyeballs locked onto mine. I don't really believe I was worried. Cheetah don't tend to attack humans, but it was taking a huge effort just to make that camera work. Don't move. Don't break the moment.

The cheetah turned away, had one more look at the herd, and crouched down again.

'Get up Noel,' I said, 'get up. It's going to happen.'

Now, I'm awfully glad, he didn't ask me how I knew it was going to happen, because I'd have had to tell him. No-one else in that van had seen my special moment; I think boredom had set in. Noel had reloaded so he brought the camera up to his shoulder again, focused on the spot where they lay and was ready. In less than a minute both cheetah stood bolt upright on those stilt-like legs, and without so much as a look back at their audience they both started into that slow rhythmical walk, their shoulders moving like two pistons in the cylinders of a mighty motor, with a huge stroke. Rising about a foot or more above their back in a seemingly effortless motion, they propelled the fastest animals on the surface of the earth forward toward their quarry. Their whole body arched and flexed like a piece of black and yellow sprung steel, coiled ready to explode. Explode it did. In an instant they went from a walk to eighty kilometres an hour. They ran between two parked vans as if they weren't even there.

The crowd erupted. It was the craziest thing I've ever experienced. We were yelling to everyone, 'Go, Go, Go, Go,' like some crazed punters cheering on the favourite at a Melbourne Cup. 'Go, Go, Go.' The wildebeest, sensing the danger, took off as well. The area erupted into a sea of dust, but the lead cheetah was far faster than his mate. He'd selected his quarry and sprang. He went up underneath the neck of the fleeing wildebeest, wrapped both front legs around the panic-stricken creature, hung on for no more than three or four seconds, and fell to the ground, with a thud.

Cheetah can only sprint for four hundred metres. They can

only do it once in every four hours; any more than that and their muscles literally turn to jelly. They are lucky to make a kill in more than one out of five chases. No cheetah in its right mind would tackle a wildebeest. They're far too big and far too heavy. Antelope are more their style.

I had witnessed a Shakespearian drama. A real live play, performed in front of an audience right in the middle of Africa. It was almost as though we were patrons at a performance, theatre-goers in a huge outdoor arena. I felt privileged to have been part of that audience.

But what about the cheetah and me? What happened in those seconds when we stood frozen, staring fixedly into one another's eyes? It was more than staring—it was reading; reading intent, reading feeling, reading what a wild animal can't say, but can do. We all talk to animals, most of us every day. G'day dog, hello cat—it's the norm. But do we take the time to listen to them. I think not. Animals talk to us all the time. It is we who do not listen, mostly because we don't stop and watch. They talk in a very different language. Theirs is one of body movements and facial expressions. That great man with horses, Monty Roberts, writes of the language of the horse, a language he calls 'equus'. It is a language that took him many years to learn. Years spent in observation and in practice, with the wild horses of the American plains. And I'll go to my grave knowing that cheetah spoke to me. There was that magical flow of energy between us when our gazes met, be it thought or what I don't know. In any case he said to me, 'Don't go away Harry, it's going to happen any minute. And I don't want you to miss it.'

Thanks pal, you're the best.

Sadly the cheetah are in a fairly precarious position. They

are amongst the most inbred of all wild animals and thus their gene pool is extremely small. The loss of fertility in the male population is becoming something of a problem. Yet with all of this and their position fairly close to the bottom of the carnivore hierarchy, they still manage to hold. Captive breeding programs are in place in many zoos, both here and overseas. Western Plains Zoo, at Dubbo in New South Wales, has quite an active breeding colony, and perhaps with the likely injection of new genetic material the wild population will get a much-needed boost. The fastest animal on the ground needs our help to stick around!

28

A Magnificent Creature

There's a place in Kenya called 'The Ark'. It's built up high in the Aberdare Mountains, surrounded by dense green jungle and swirling silvery mists. It's so called because it looks exactly like the thing Noah launched all those thousands of years ago. But it is different in one special way. You see at 'The Ark' the animals are on the outside; it's the people who are on the inside. The place is a very special motel. It caters exclusively to those tourists intent on viewing Africa's amazing animals in their natural state. You've gotta be inside well before sunset, for it's then that they lock the doors. It's the animals that get priority treatment here. You can spend that time taking a walk on many of the viewing platforms that stretch out into the jungle for a first-hand look at the amazing bird life that lives high up in the forest canopy.

The building is set up very much like a modern-day motel complex—dormitory rooms line the lower levels, each one with a small porthole for outside viewing. They're equipped with everything you need, and that includes a buzzer, fitted immediately above your bed. There's a series of signals. One buzz means antelope or something similar. Two buzzes means elephants, rhinos, the big guys. Three buzzes is all action, lions, leopards, or cheetah. On the floor above there are dining areas, conference rooms and a beautifully relaxing lounge area heated by a massive fire. So why the fire? Well, although we are near the equator, we are also at a very high altitude and it gets pretty chilly when the sun goes down, even in the middle of summer.

There is a cleared patch on the jungle floor at the sharp end of 'The Ark'. It's a large salt pan. For an area of about two hundred metres immediately in front the undergrowth has been cleared away and the animals have easy access to this large open space. Salt is something that attracts almost all herbivores. At night they come in—sometimes one at a time, and at others in herds. You can be lucky or you can be stiff; we were lucky. The sun had set and the sounds of the jungle were all around. We were pretty high up and looking down. Floodlight illuminated the scene. The first to arrive were some large Hartebeest, a little unsure at first but slowly they ventured into the floodlit area. As cameras started to roll the animals seemed totally unperplexed by being the centre of attention. Some other small deer, even a couple of monkeys, made their presence felt. They behaved as if everything was totally normal. We posed no threat.

Then we saw an elephant. First one, then another, and another. Until finally there were nearly a dozen. Boy, this was sensational. You had a chance to watch the social behaviour and the interaction between the various members of the herd. It was pretty obvious that the older female was in charge.

It was time for dinner, I bolted it down in a hurry. When we returned their numbers had swollen to some thirty-five! There were elephants everywhere. Big ones, little ones and lame ones. Their language was fascinating. Long soft low rumblings, interspersed with funny little squeaks. Trunks swaying backwards and forwards in a rhythmical fashion, occasionally raised or thrown over their backs in a mock salute. Milling around, the mature female intent on keeping her herd in order. Two of the younger elephants were lame on one front leg and it seemed to me that they had probably each broken their elbow. The front leg hung pretty uselessly by each of their sides and it was with great difficulty that they dragged the huge weights around. I'd have liked to have helped them. Lots of the other youngsters tended to pick on these two: goading them, pushing and bullying them. Incredibly, the females in the herd seemed to pick up on what was going on. They pushed the youngsters towards the centre of the group protecting them from the onslaught of the troublemakers. It seemed almost as though one or more of the females had been assigned the duty of babysitter, for it didn't matter where the herd moved to, either in or out of the clearing, the less fortunate youngsters were always kept in the centre of the group.

A young bull elephant tried to join the herd. Charging in from the surrounding jungle, he trumpeted his presence, and made towards the herd, now intent on enjoying the taste of their salt lick. He was greeted by a mock charge from the matriarch, and driven off into the scrub. He made a good three or four more attempts, some more subtle and some downright forceful, but was chased away on each occasion by the matriarch. The males within the group seemed really just to wander around and do very little. Every time there was any sort of ruction within the herd and in particular with the youngsters it was the females who stepped in to settle things down. Strangely, there wasn't a great deal of trumpeting or carrying on, instead most of the noise was this low grumbling sort of sound that elephants tend to make when they're busy, and content with the world. We stayed half the night—and so did they.

You meet lots of different characters in Africa and game wardens are a breed of their own. The problem these days is, that now having established wildlife parks, we need to manage them. Gone are the days when the animals were free to roam the plains of Africa. These days the poacher's bullet has meant the only way to save so many species from extinction is to lock them up behind closed doors. Well probably not doors, but rather, behind wire fences. In so doing, while we may have protected them, we've also prevented a great deal of interaction between groups, not only in the sense of breeding but also in the social scaffold of life. Lions, for instance, have become problems in some areas. They've learnt that they can hunt far more efficiently if they chase their prey against a cyclone fence which borders the park. Elephants in other areas have bred without predation and their numbers have grown out of all proportion. How do we manage a situation like this? For manage it we must; we are the very people who created the status quo and all the problems that go with it.

Controlling a captive animal population like this means in fact playing 'God' to all the species that live within the park. That means unfortunately that some animals must be culled.

'What,' I said to my warden friend in his slouch hat and khaki uniform, with the heavy bore rifle slung over his shoulder, resting neatly on his frame, 'is the animal that you hate to cull most?'

'No question about it,' he said. 'Elephants.'

'Because they're so big,' I said.

'No, because they're so much like us.'

Their social strata, their welfare system, their care for one another, all of these are human attributes. The elephant is so much like us, or rather, perhaps we should be a lot more like the elephant. These days as I look back through my photographs of the time spent in Africa this thought comes back to me over and over. They are the largest mammal walking the surface of the earth. They do it with so much dignity, so much strength and with so much pride. What a tragedy it is that we should seek to kill such a magnificent creature for the sake of a trinket. It really is just a sample of off-white jewellery, or perhaps an ornament gathering dust on the shelf, or a chess piece, carved from the once-living tissue of such a gentle creature. To me it is unthinkable. Have you seen the orphaned baby elephants? I have. So lonely and so lost they look. How do such little animals understand? How do they ever trust man again? The ivory trade and all the graft that goes with it needs to be buried forever. It is only when we make a stand against the sale of such supposed treasures that things will come to an end and the elephants of Africa will roam without fear the wilds of that massive continent.

29

Monkey Business

Most people are fascinated by monkeys. I reckon many of us can recognise some vague likeness to a long-lost relation in the faces of these incredibly active and very perceptive primates. I particularly like orang-utans, gibbons, and the spider monkeys.

Being in television, you're often afforded the luxury of going places and doing things that other people just can't do. It's a privilege I don't take lightly. And when it comes to animals, the closer I can get the better I like it. This story takes place in a zoo, I can't say where, and I can't say when. I wouldn't want anyone to get into trouble. But the story, my friends, is absolutely true.

I had half a day to spare between filming segments for 'Talk to the Animals' and had struck up a pretty good rapport with the head primate keeper, with whom I'd been working closely the previous day. There we were, the two of us, in the orang enclosure first thing in the morning, busy hiding food. I often wonder what the orangs thought was going on. Never mind the general public who seemed to gaze with some awe at these two apparent idiots stuffing nuts and fruit under logs, into holes, behind rocks, under grass and anywhere else we thought might make a good hidey hole. Talk about role reversal. But it was fun. We spent two hours hiding what it took the orangs twenty minutes to find. But after all, their nose is much better than ours and no, they weren't watching.

This sort of therapy, by the way, is very necessary for all wild animals in zoos. Prevention of boredom in zoos is a major problem. Take the polar bears, for example. These animals are kept entirely out of their natural habitat. In an artificial environment of concrete and fibreglass they struggle to pass the day without developing serious behavioural problems. Things like pacing and licking become so entrenched in their day-to-day routine as to be accepted as normal, although they're far from it. Many zoos have devised ways of overcoming the problems. In the wild, animals have to search and hunt for their food. Mother nature doesn't serve it up to them on a dish the way we used to feed them. In many zoos polar bears' food is mainly fish presented in a huge block of ice. The bears play with this in the water like some massive toy and in time, of course, it melts and they access their meal a bit at a time. As well as making them work for their tucker, it provides a source of amusement as well.

Singapore Zoo has gone one step further and if you ever get a chance to visit this fantastic establishment don't miss it. The polar bears here can be viewed from behind huge glass windows. And, on a regular basis throughout the day, they receive a token feed of live fish. Their water is chilled to a near natural environmental temperature and it is absolutely sensational to see these huge animals coursing their fishy quarry between the artificial icebergs. The zoo has other exhibits too where the animals are made to work for their food. The big cats of South America get to swim and fish for their dinner as well. All their food ends up in a running stream and they must take the plunge if they fancy a feed. There are a lot of lessons here for our own domestic animals. Food is always the best reward for any activity and toys that provide this sort of reward incentive such as Buster Cubes and Kongs are amongst the best you can give your animals to keep them occupied for hours while you are away from home. I look at it this way: people play the pokies because every so often they get a little reward—and of course there is always the chance of a big one! Animals are no different. They will keep playing as long as their interest is maintained, and food is the best way to maintain it.

Anyway, to return to the orangs, they seemed happy that they'd discovered all of their tucker in pretty quick time. You can sit and watch these guys for hours; they really are great time-wasters, but time was something I was running out of.

'Anything else you'd like to see?' my guide asked.

'Sure, got any gibbons?'

'Yeah,' he said, 'come on down.'

I really like gibbons. They are one sensational animal. Their enclosure was a really old one. It was made from thick iron bars covered with a heavy mesh of chain wire. The whole thing had been painted black all over and resembled something like the standard zoo housing of the 1950s. It was very high and fairly big too, but with the usual cement floor and rendered shelter area. Pretty austere! We went around the back. That's where all the action is. And that's where there was no chain wire either. So I sat down alongside the big steel bars. In a flash the leader of the troop was there. Hands straight out, grabbed the cap from my head and away. Fair dinkum the little bloke took me completely by surprise—and the keeper too. Round and round the enclosure he went. Swinging the cap like some trophy from the final of a major football game. Showing off to all and sundry for at least ten minutes.

'You can kiss that goodbye,' my guide announced.

Well, I reckoned, it was only one cap. He obviously needed

it more than me. After all, I did have another fifty-four at home, so what the heck! It was getting a bit tattered around the edges anyhow.

Then the most incredible thing happened. At the end of ten minutes he came back down to where I was sitting, pushed the cap out through the bars and tried to put it back on my head. My guide stood there open mouthed. Wow! I gave him a hand. That was a mistake. He grabbed my hand with his and yanked it firmly into the cage.

'You'll get bitten, you'll get bitten.' And I had been once before and yeah, they hurt, but I somehow felt that it wasn't going to happen today. He pulled and he pulled and for a little animal he was incredibly strong. So I slid along the rough wooden seat till the whole of my arm was inside the enclosure. He let go and moved closer to sit alongside me. I left my arm where it was. He put his face to the bars. I put mine there too. There we sat, cheek to cheek, man and monkey, listening and talking to one another for twenty minutes, totally oblivious to anything that may have been going on around us.

I've spoken to many people in my life, some dead boring, and others totally fascinating, but I have to tell you that this was one of the most meaningful conversations I have ever had. I don't understand one word of gibbon, and I'm sure he couldn't understand me. But we both shared a common language, a language of understanding and patience that, if you have the time, it's possible to have with any animal, anywhere. This had to be one of the best moments of my life. Even now as I write about it I re-experience that incredible feeling of being just so close to a wild animal, so close that you have their trust. You have to believe it. Electric, sensational, stunning and at the same time terribly humbling.

Planes don't wait however; it was time to go and I pulled away and walked back around the front of the enclosure. He started to cry. What do you do? I cried too, and back I went. Took the cap off this time and we sat again for another ten minutes. We were just so close, I could feel his breath, and the gentle fur of his face on mine. Ah, my little friend, you are so small and I so big and yet you would still be my friend, I thought. One look in his face said 'yes'. This time I really did have to go. The airport was quite a distance away.

As we walked away up the long asphalt ramp that led from the enclosure I turned back, and something tugged terribly hard at the strings of my heart. For there he was, right at the very top of his steel and concrete prison, his arms stretched out through the wire screaming, begging, pleading with me to come back.

'Geez,' I said with a very definite quaver in my voice, 'it's a bloody tragedy.'

'You don't know half the tragedy,' the keeper said.

'Whadda ya mean?' says dumb ol' me.

'Well, it's like this,' he said. 'In the next twenty or thirty years the only gibbons you're likely to see will be the ones in zoos.' With that he got pretty darn angry.

'People like your Prime Minister,' he exploded, 'who spend all that money on fancy furniture. Well, it's people like them who buy all those teak tables, and all those chairs ... well those are the trees my gibbons used to play in.'

Now he was crying too. I put my hand on his shoulder and we walked away in silence.

But you see it's not just his gibbons, my dear friends, but mine and yours too, and your children's, and your children's children's. The animals of this world belong to us all. The rate at which we are decimating the jungles on this planet is something that will indict the human race for an eternity. Leave the trees alone. Leave the gibbons their home. They were here before us and God knows they deserve to be here long after we are gone.

That cap is something special. It was yours for such a short while. I wear it no more, it's too special for that. I miss you my little friend—and all I can do is to hope that in some small way I can do something to redress the balance that is so obviously weighted against you. Let us all try!

TV House Calls

30

A Special Place

'Harry's Practice' is filmed to a very large degree in Tasmania. I utilise a veterinary clinic in Launceston, which caters mainly for small animals and that means anything from dogs and cats down to birds, mice, guinea pigs and rabbits. We fitted the surgery out in such a way that the clients felt comfortable in what was a very 'James Herriot' sort of environment. The windows and the cupboards received a make-over from a set producer, and sound damping was installed in the ceiling as were special lights and reflectors. The pictures on the walls are, in the main, from my personal collection; I'm a bit of an Anglophile you see, and enjoy collecting a lot of old memorabilia from the mother country. In fact, most of this stuff I gathered in the two years I spent working in and around the English countryside.

The clients that come through the door don't really expect to be on television, although in a city the size of Lonnie word gets around pretty quickly. I used to reckon that Tassie had the most active grapevine in the world. But it's also the most inaccurate! Picture this: a young lady with her mum sitting quietly in the corner of the waiting room. On her lap, wrapped in a small white hand towel, is her favourite pet. There we are: producer, two cameramen, a sound recordist and me. Pretty imposing, I reckon. It was usually my job to ask if the client minded being on television. You have to pay people that courtesy. We just don't barge in—that wouldn't be fair or ethical.

'Would you like to be on 'Harry's Practice'?' I asked her.
'Absolutely,' she said.
'Well, what have you got in there?' I asked.
She said, 'It's my pet rat and I want to have it put to sleep.'
Strike, I thought to myself. 'Are you sure?' I asked.
'Oh yes,' she said, very assuredly. 'And I want to do it on TV too.'
'Why?' I asked.
'Because,' this fifteen-year-old replied, 'I want to be a vet like you one day.'
'But you don't have to be on TV to be a vet,' I explained.
'No,' she agreed, 'but I want people to see what happens to an animal when it's put to sleep.'

She was one very determined and very self-assured young lady.

None of us were sure how this would all go let alone just how you the viewers would react to the story. But there's no harm in trying, so that's what we did.

You don't see anybody wearing a microphone on the show. That's because they're hidden. Mine is in the very peak of the cap and the cable runs down the back of my neck to the transmitter around my waist. Steve, my 'soundo', miked my young client up as well, and checked that he could hear us both. We were ready to go. Her mum was coming in too for a bit of moral support, but she wasn't going to be part of the conversation so we left her in mute mode.

My consulting table is some twenty-five centimetres higher than a normal bench. The reason is simple. Most animals at normal table height would be a long way from my face and from a photographic point of view the closer the animal gets to my ageing dial the better, because the photographic field can then become very much smaller and the subject that much bigger. Besides, it stops me bending over all the time. I guess this is the reason that most people who see me off the screen are surprised at my height. Television has the habit of shortening and widening just about everybody. I'm actually six feet one. Some even tell me I look younger off the set. We never wear any make-up; what you see is what you get.

Anyhow, in we all walked, the two cameras started to roll and the producer and Steve sat in another room outside and watched and listened to the whole thing on a monitor. My young client, spread a towel on the table and popped her rat onto it. The reason for its imminent demise was pretty damn obvious. The poor little guy had a massive tumour on the side of its chest—half again as big as its head.

Rats and mice do get a lot of tumours. They are sometimes malignant, but more often than not simply grow rapidly in size, creating massive problems for these great little pets.

It's often difficult to explain to clients about the relative size of lumps. A mere trifle on a dog could be a life or death situation for a budgie. So I generally look at lumps relative to the size of the animal's head, and ask my clients to imagine how they'd feel carrying around a lump even half the size of their own head. Imagine then the load that this poor rat was carrying around. His young owner had made up her mind quite some time ago that this would have to be the end for her whiskered friend. She had been down the path before and knew just what sort of life expectancy these rodents had. She had plenty more at home but I somehow got the feeling that this little guy in front of me was something special to her.

◆

The act of putting an animal to sleep is called euthanasia. The procedure is accomplished with a simple injection of a concentrated dose of an anaesthetic agent. But it is something which I never undertake lightly. As a vet we are given the power to administer drugs that are capable of taking life. That, my friends, is a pretty onerous responsibility. Who gives me the power of life or death over other living, breathing things? Is it God? If so, then I respect that power. I treat it with a type of awe.

We spoke for a minute about the value of life, her love of animals and the fate of this little creature now looking somewhat inquisitively around the room. Was she sure? Did she really want to stay? The answer to all this was a very definite 'yes'! The drug was drawn up into a fine syringe, and injected into the abdomen of the rat. It would be far too traumatic on the animal to have struggled with a vein. They are far too tiny and the stress of immobilising the little guy I thought too much, for both him and all concerned. Right through, the cameras were rolling on her, on the rat, on me and on her mum. We talked calmly and quietly about our philosophies on life. Where do dead animals go? Do they have a spirit? Is there an afterlife for our friends? These are pretty deep and meaningful questions, particularly for a teenager.

The drug is absorbed very quickly, and it took no more than sixty seconds for the rat to slowly curl up and quietly go to sleep. The atmosphere in the room was incredible. You can't describe the feelings unless you're part of that situation. As the rat breathed its last and lay there quietly on the towel, I began to fold the corners slowly over the lifeless form. First one, then the second, the third and the last.

Something made me look up for a second, and as I did I caught a tear trickling down the face of her mum. The young girl followed my gaze, and she too turned around, saw her mum crying, and then she too burst into tears. It was all a bit much for me as well, and I too started to cry. I'm not ashamed of that, I do it all the time. Then from over my left shoulder came the most hysterical sobbing you've ever heard. My senior cameraman was in full flood, the heavy Betacam rocking up and down on his shoulder as he struggled to fight back the tears. The producer, who'd been watching all of this from the other room, burst in demanding to know what was going wrong with the camera. By this stage everybody except the producer was in tears.

'Get out of here,' we yelled, almost as one.

'What's going on?' he asked. 'What are you all crying for?'

Why were four grown men, a woman and a teenager sobbing their hearts out over one little rat? You had to be there. If you hadn't been there, you couldn't know. Anyhow, crying does you good. We all felt better, except the producer of course, who walked away scratching his head. And y'know, we often talk about what happened in those few minutes in the surgery that day and he's still at a loss to understand the emotion of the whole experience.

But there is an end to this story. I promised that I would take the little guy home and bury him in our special garden. And everyone concerned thought this would be a fitting end for him. It was a beautiful sunny afternoon and, as I've related elsewhere, this special plot sits atop a hill looking out over most of our farm. We'd picked it on purpose. You can see it from the house. Anyway, the producer thought the garden plot presented a pleasing end to the story, at least from a visual aspect.

I buried the little rat near the edge on the southern side, underneath a Cecile Brunner rose, and alongside an echidna and a pet rabbit. Funny collection, isn't it? But then people who love animals really don't seem to care too much about what they are or what they may look like. As long as they're alive, and can react in some small way, then that'll do.

We mounded the earth over the grave and placed a small red anemone over the site. The idea was that we'd start with a close-up shot of the grave and gradually reveal the whole garden and the scene beyond. It would be truly beautiful. To achieve it we needed a device called a crane, or a jib arm. It's really a see-saw with the camera at one end, some weights counterbalancing the other and a swinging pivot in the centre. The senior cameraman, poor ol' fella, was again in charge of the shot. By gradually pulling down on the weights he could elevate the camera from the grave site to the vista beyond.

'Well,' said my boss, the producer, 'I want you to say a few words, mate, while we tilt up.'

'What sorta thing?'

'Oh, you know, just about life and death and all that kind of stuff.'

'Okay, no worries.'

I've knelt down alongside the grave, camera rolling, and away we go. We're no more than ten seconds into the dialogue when the cameraman calls a halt. Take 2. Same thing, same problem. Take 3. Again ten seconds only. Take 4. Just as bad. 'What in God's name is going on mate?' I asked.

'Why don't you damn well shut up,' he said. 'The way you're going on about all this stuff, I get that many tears in my eyes I can't even see.'

He's a great bloke, my cameraman, looks pretty tough

on the outside, but on the inside, he's a really sensitive guy. Eventually we did the take. I kept my mouth shut, and he got the pictures. You couldn't see my lips anyhow, so I recorded the voiceover after and we married the two together and everybody was happy.

I often think of this story and although we went out a day or two later to the girl's home and filmed what must have been nearly fifty rats, if you count the babies, that surgery episode will live with me forever. Such a small animal, but such a large outpouring of emotion and grief. It is never the size of the animal, it is the size of our attachment that really counts. I walk past that garden nearly every day that I'm home, and y'know some days I stop, only for a minute, but that's all it takes to remember a wonderful little animal and an owner who, for all her young years, had a genuine love and, what's more, an understanding of the animals in her care. If you love animals the way she did, you won't go too far wrong in life.

31

A Very Small Operation

All the cases that you see in the Launceston surgery are just as they happen. We don't organise any of them or orchestrate what goes on. But it's important in any television show to try and present not only information but entertainment as well. The buzzword in the industry is 'infotainment'. Drama is an important element in any production but that's something that you can't arrange, it just happens. When it does, you've got to grab it with both hands, run with it and tidy up the loose ends later.

It's Thursday night, 6.30 p.m., flat out, waiting room chockers, dogs, cats and people everywhere. You walk from the calm of the consulting room to the mayhem in the front office. 'He's choking, he's choking,' screams the woman in the corner.

'Who's choking?' I yell.

'Bandit, Bandit. Bandit's choking.'

There's a real element of panic in her voice. In all this pandemonium someone has to keep a clear head. No time for elaborate microphones and all that rubbish, just swing the pole with the big mike over their heads and hope for the best. Camera's rolling, let's get on with it.

'Well you'd better come in,' I said.

Bandit was choking all right. Sitting on the table, head in the air, as if willing the Lord to pour more oxygen down his poor congested windpipe. Gasping, wheezing and getting bluer by the minute.

'What's happened?' I said.

'He's swallowed an earring.'

'He's swallowed a what?'

'He's swallowed an earring. He was running along the top of my dressing table and he swallowed an earring. Well, I think he has.'

Bandit was a black and white rat! So named because the little bugger was always stealing things.

This was a dead-set emergency. Without immediate intervention we would be looking at a very dead rat.

'He'll need oxygen straightaway. I'll whip him down to the hospital and then we'll get an X-ray.'

Have you ever tried to open a rat's mouth? Apart from the fact that you're probably going to get very badly bitten, you can't open it far enough to see over the back of their tongue. Anatomically speaking, it's impossible. So there's no way I was going to get a look around the larynx, the back of the throat and all those associated structures. But an X-ray should show up any metallic object and most earrings that I'm familiar with have enough metal in them to be plainly visible. Things like wood just don't show. But an X-ray would have to wait until I got this guy away from the life-and-death precipice he was balancing on.

The anaesthetic machine can be specially modified to administer gases to small animals like birds and rodents. I put him on pure oxygen with a little mask over his face and immediately the little bludger turned the corner. However, a rat confined to an anaesthetic mask becomes an unhappy rat in a very short period of time, and unhappy rats demonstrate their unhappiness by biting anything and everything in sight. Unfortunately, my fingers were the nearest objects. A few muttered words under the breath. This wasn't going to be easy. So I ran a bit of anaesthetic gas in with the oxygen as well. The tips of two of my fingers were now bleeding profusely, which made it difficult to grasp things—and they were damn sore as well. After four or five minutes of breathing in the sweet smelling isofluorane, he was sound asleep. Peace at last, thank heavens for that. We wheeled in the portable X-ray machine, snapped off a couple of pictures of his torso, developed the film and guess what? Not a sign of any foreign material anywhere in his system. Back up to the client.

'Are you sure he swallowed an earring?'

'Oh well, I can't be certain, but he was playing around with these feathery things I've got and then suddenly he started to choke.'

'Did you actually see him swallow it?'

'No, not actually. But I think he did.'

Well feathers, that could explain it. You don't see feathers on an X-ray, and perhaps it was just a small bit of feather that Bandit swallowed and it got stuck in his throat. So back down to the surgery we go. As soon as we took Bandit off the anaesthetic machine he started to asphyxiate again. In fact within thirty seconds he'd go completely blue and again be on the point of choking to death. It was time for dramatic action. I figured there just had to be something caught at the very top of his windpipe. I couldn't access it through the mouth, there was only one course of action left. I'd have to cut his throat.

We call it a tracheotomy. It's a lifesaving procedure in cases of tracheal obstruction. Back under anaesthetic we go. Bandit was rolled on his back, no time for all the fancy clipping, scrubbing, disinfecting and all that muckin' about. This was real emergency stuff. I swabbed the skin with a little antiseptic and drew the scalpel down the whole length of the underside of the neck—quite a long cut. This exposed the windpipe. There was virtually no bleeding, so I lifted it clear of the surrounding tissues, and made a cut halfway through the tube.

There's not a great deal of difference between what we call the trachea in most animals. It's basically a tube strengthened by circular rings of cartilage that conveys air from the larynx to the lungs. What I did was to cut in and through one of these rings opening up the tube to the outside atmosphere and bypassing the larynx. Bandit immediately breathed with ease, through the hole I'd created. There was only one problem. He wasn't getting any anaesthetic, so he woke up. He sure was angry. By the time we got halfway through the procedure I had bite marks on every finger bar one, and was finding surgery just that bit more difficult. So we had to work in between. He'd have a good dose of anaesthetic gas, we'd stop for thirty seconds, work like fury, and then connect him up before he woke up and started biting again. Who said working with animals was easy?

What I needed was a tube, or a flexible probe, that I could run from my incision in the trachea back up towards the larynx pushing anything that might be stuck up and out through the mouth.

'Give me some tubes,' I said to the nurse.

Quick as a flash she arrived with a great fistful. They were either too small and too limp to do the job, or too thick and too rigid to push up. Things were getting desperate. This little guy's life was literally in the balance.

'Haven't you got anything else?' I asked. My fingers were starting to hurt. 'There must be more. Go and have a look.'

She shuffled off without a word and returned with another collection. One at a time I sifted through this lot as well, all the while juggling Bandit between the anaesthetic machine and the atmosphere. I was getting pretty close. Just needed something a fraction bigger. And all the time, don't forget, the cameras were recording the whole event.

'Give me the next one up,' I said.

'I can't, I can't.'

'Why can't ya? Give me the next one!' I was more than a little agitated. 'Give me the next one!!!'

'I can't.'

'Why can't ya?'

'I can't see.'

'Why can't ya see?'

Well dear readers, at this moment I finally looked up from my patient and there stood my poor nurse. What a sorry sight, tears rolling down her cheeks, her face red and swollen like an overripe Grosse Lisse tomato. Her hands too were red and swollen.

'What in heavens name is wrong with you?' I asked.

'I don't know, I don't know,' she said. 'I think I'm allergic to rats.' And sure enough she was.

Well we did finally manage to get the situation stabilised, and by using a larger, stiffer tube I did feel that I was able to make breathing a lot easier for poor old Bandit. There was no sign of a feather or anything like that, so the cause of the sudden bout of asphyxiation remained a mystery. The tracheotomy incision was sutured open to enable Bandit to breathe through the hole I'd created while his larynx had time to repair. He spent the night in hospital just to make sure we didn't get a recurrence.

This story has a happy ending. Bandit went home with his throat still cut, breathing happily through the hole until it closed and the problem resolved itself. I'll never know what caused the obstruction but perhaps that's just as well. But I've learnt one thing from the whole episode. In the future, when I interview prospective staff, I'll make sure their allergies are to things like privet and wattle, and not to rats and mice.

32

Surprise Visits

I love making surprise house calls, and I know from your letters that you all love them too. It's a concept we came up with right at the very start of the show. Believe you me, they are genuine surprises. We travel all over Australia and fair dinkum, people don't know we're coming. We just turn up on their doorstep.

It goes something like this. Perth's our target. So we put a little ad in the local paper saying simply that Dr Harry will be coming to Perth in the near future and if you've got a problem you'd like him to come and solve, then please fax, email or write to the production office in Sydney. Sometimes we get overwhelmed and in the case of Perth just recently nearly five hundred letters arrived on our desk. Then it's the job of the researchers to get stuck in. A couple of girls who are pretty cluey at sifting what sounds like good television material from the ordinary, plough through all your letters to find just the right sort of problem that will be both informative and entertaining. Usually they get it pretty right. It's then up to the producer and myself to narrow the field even further. Then it's jump on a plane, black bag in hand, and away we go.

Everybody who writes gets a reply, although it's obviously impossible for me to reply to every letter in person. We do our best. The day dawns and we're out on the road, usually by at least eight o'clock. It pays to start pretty early because we do like to catch people when they're home, and often before they go to work or weekends are the best time. There are generally two or three calls in the same area. Then it is just a case of knocking on doors until finally we catch someone at home. We never tell them we're coming. We just turn up.

A drive up and down the street with me crouching in the back out of view to suss out the best approach to the front door is essential. In television, light is very important and the cameraman needs to know exactly where the shadows fall so he can be prepared when I knock on that front door. We park down the road out of sight and get set up. Microphone in the old tweed cap, with cord running down the back of the neck to a transmitter on my belt. Time only for a quick test of the equipment. Trusty black bag and stethoscope always in the left hand, letter or fax in the right. Ready. Set. Let's go. And away we scoot down the street and up to the door. Cameras rolling all the while. Cameraman and soundo right behind me, producer watching the whole thing from a distance, so as not to get in the way. Now folks, this is where it really gets interesting.

Knock, knock.

'G'day.'

'Oh, g'day.'

'I'm Dr Harry.'

'Yeah, I know who you are.'

'Well I've come to look at the barking dog.'

'Oh, he's just over the road. He barks all the time.'

'No, I've come to look at YOUR barking dog.'

'I haven't got a barking dog.'

'But it says here in this letter that you have.'

'Oh, that's mum's dog.'

'Well, where's mum?'

'Oh, she's not in.'

'Well what about the dog?'

'Oh, yeah, he's in.'

'Well can I come in?'

'Oh, yeah. Hey I thought you guys were doing a raid.'

'What d'ya mean, doing a raid?'

'Well there's this amphetamine factory just down the street, and I thought you guys had come to bust it.'

'No way. The dog'll do me.'

Boy, oh, boy what an effort just to get in the front door. But it was worth it. He was a great little dog. Just couldn't stand the telephone ringing or the garbage disposal unit under the sink in full swing. He'd bark, he'd bite and he'd jump up and down. We fixed that one, no worries. Being a terrier of sorts made him very smart and absolutely easy to train. It was simply a matter of having him under control, and rewarding him for being good, whilst you turned on the various sounds that upset the dog. Usually we spend around two to three hours at each call. It really does take a long time to put the whole thing together. Roughly speaking, in situations like this it takes around forty minutes of work at the scene to make one minute of television. We took our time with this little bloke and at the end he was behaving himself like a real champ.

Then there was the dear old soul with a cat problem. The letter made really interesting reading. The cat had some horrid skin disease that had defied treatment for some five or six years and by the sound of things this old puss was just about on its last legs.

Knock, knock. I see someone faintly at the back of a long corridor.

'Anyone home? Anyone home?'

'Coming,' was the faint reply.

She shuffled up the corridor.

'You're not filming me, are you?'

We were of course, we film everything.

'I haven't got me teeth in.'

That was obvious. She had the gummiest grin I had ever seen.

'Can I come in?'

She finally got to the screen door after shuffling the whole length of the corridor.

'Yes, yes do come in.'

The cameraman and soundo followed us down the corridor and into the kitchen. The whole place was so dark it was like the inside of an Egyptian pyramid.

'You're not filming me are you?'

We were.

The kitchen was an absolute disaster. Every horizontal surface was covered with little tin dishes. The bench tops, the kitchen table, the chairs, you name it, everywhere were these damned dishes. I'm no expert when it comes to cooking but they sure looked like the sort of things you'd cook a meat pie in. Heaven only knows what was in them. There were hundreds of them, all laid out, all over the place. The joint was in semi-darkness, not a light in sight, and the more I looked the more of these wretched dishes seemed to be lying around, all with this funny sort of brown, granular material in them.

'You're not filming me are ya?'

We were.

'I can't find me teeth,' she continued.

'Where's the cat?' I enquired.

She took absolutely no notice. I repeated myself in a considerably louder voice. Again no response. Instead she was now

proceeding to stack one dish on top of another till the whole pile began to take on the appearance of some huge wobbling mountain of plates.

'You're really not filming this are ya?'

We were.

She never found her teeth but the whole damn pile of dishes slipped from her grasp and crashed to the floor around us. I was in mortal danger. This lady was a dead-set disaster. Heaven help the cat, no wonder it had problems.

All efforts to help retrieve the dishes from the floor were met with a firm negative. There she was on her hands and knees, crawling around in all of this funny brown stuff, still with her teeth out, gathering up the dishes.

Well, after another five minutes we did find the cat. The poor animal had taken refuge behind the kitchen dresser. It seemed scared out of his wits by the time we finally did extricate him and manage to get a look at this supposed skin problem.

Now, not all that we do goes to air. And this one didn't. But I always follow up and make sure that the animal receives the attention it deserves. This cat had a major skin problem—and living in the atmosphere which had already brought me to the verge of distress was surely having the same effect on the cat. It couldn't stop licking itself. Treatment was prescribed and away we went.

Some cases sound so interesting we actually make two or three attempts to catch up with the owner. Saturday morning. Eight o'clock. From about ten kilometres away we give a quick phonecall, just to make sure. Someone answers. We hang up straightaway. Someone's home. Get set up. Knock on the door. No-one home! Just the dog barking. The dog's no good without the owner. Ring again that afternoon. No answer. But the problem sounds so good we're going to give it one more try. It's Sunday morning, seven forty-five. A bit early for most people. Not for us. We're sure to catch someone at home. No phone call this time. Just turn up. We'd been here before and knew the routine. Up to the door and a very loud knock. Dog barks. We wait. Knock again. Dog keeps barking and then the door opens. 'Oh! Hell ...'

Yeah. I saw how she looked and could only imagine how she

felt. What a mess. But that's the way a lot of young ladies look the morning after a very enjoyable ball the night before. It was her parents' dog and they'd left to go fishing only five minutes after our first call the day before. You can be unlucky sometimes, but somehow this young lady reckoned she was far more unlucky than we were. Still, to smooth things over she was gracious enough to make us all a cup of tea and sit and enjoy a little breakfast with us. Well, after she'd made herself a bit more presentable at least.

Sundays seem to be our best days. I've caught them in their pyjamas and in their nighties. And to date, everyone's been pretty good about the situation. One bloke didn't answer the knock on his door. Didn't seem to matter how hard I knocked. Nobody stirred. I hadn't rung and it was 7.30 a.m. so we used the mobile. I could hear his phone ringing inside and was about to give up when suddenly it was answered. There had to be someone at home. I knocked loudly. 'Hang on. There's somebody at the door,' came the voice from inside. While my producer, who was obviously an actress in her former life, continued her meaningless conversation with my victim, he opened the door, bleary eyed and clutching at the drawstring of his sagging pyjamas. 'Jeez,' he said. 'I've been up all night watching the cricket.'

But what a top bloke he turned out to be. And he had a terrific dog as well. I swanned into the kitchen at the suggestion of the cameraman and made a cuppa for us both while he got changed and made himself a bit more presentable. Even the local paper turned up to do a story on our house call routine and they couldn't have happened along on a better day. Mind you, it took some effort to get a urine sample. All the neighbours thought it quite hysterical the way I was walking down the street with frying pan in hand trying to collect a few precious drops before the dog put his foot in it and up-ended the whole lot. But we got the urine, the paper got their story and the dog got fixed as well. A good day's work.

Sometimes the patient is missing altogether. Old house. Saturday morning. Joint looks a mess. Lawn hasn't been mowed for a year. Big old front verandah with partly rotting floorboards. Huge front door with leadlight features. Big loud door knocker. We're rolling. Man opens door.

'G'day I'm Dr Harry.'

'Yes,' he drawls in a sleepy voice.

'I'm here to see the young lady.' (Don't worry folks she was eight years old.)

'Oh, she's sick.'

'No I'm not Dad, who is it?'

Child appears at front door in dressing gown, not looking too sick at all. But she will be if she doesn't put a few more clothes on, it's freezing.

'Dr Harry, Dr Harry.' The eyes light up. 'You've come, you've come.'

Now I might add here that the date on the letter was some five weeks prior to the visit.

'I've come to see Patches. How is he?'

'Oh, he's dead.'

Look of despair on my face. Translated rapidly into words. 'What happened?'

'The cat ate him.'

You can't win 'em all. And I certainly can't look at a mouse once it's inside a cat. However there was an upside to the visit

243

because the remaining mice got a good veterinary going-over while I was there and they were all fit and well. As for the cat, well he spent most of the time looking in the sunroom window at these little rodents tearing round the floor, with what I can only describe as some sort of hypnotic expression on his face. So near and yet so far, I'm sure he thought.

I've surprised them in shopping centres. I've surprised them at the hairdressers. You never quite know when I'm going to turn up next. I've even turned up at the wrong address on occasions. But to turn up and find the patient has moved house is another experience again.

Up the stairs to the third floor of the units. It's Sunday morning. Coupla knocks. And the door cracks open.

'G'day. I'm here to see Tweetie.' (Well, that'll do for a name. We don't want to give too much away do we?) 'Oh, Tweetie doesn't live here now.'

'Well, where the devil is he?'

'He's on holidays.'

'He's on what?'

'He's on holidays. He always goes up to our friend's place when we go away and we're just about to go.'

Talk about a mixed-up family. No wonder the bird had problems. Didn't know whether he was Arthur or Martha. Fixed that one. He was definitely an Arthur. Trouble was, at one place they were night owls and kept him up all night watching TV. At the other home they were fowls, and all went to bed pretty soon after the sun went down. The poor bird's time clock was so disorganised he wasn't sure just when he should moult. So he fixed that, as only a bird can, and moulted all the time. Which meant that he couldn't whistle—and if this is sounding complicated to you, imagine how a brain the size of a bird's manages to cope with it.

We've had our share of nutty dogs too. Sometimes you can be unlucky. Big wide street, big front gardens. Hard to park out of sight. First call of the day, but we're running a bit late. Almost 8.30 a.m. We're just getting organised when a car drives out of the very house we're interested in. What bad luck. Not to worry. We'll give it a go anyway. Up to the door, cameras rolling, the door's open, wide open. I walk in.

Knock.

'Anyone home, anyone home?'

'You can't come in.'

'Too bad. I'm already in.'

And suddenly this partly clothed female form streaks across the corridor in front of me.

'See you in the kitchen,' I say.

Well at least the dogs were happy to see me. They were jumping all over me. It took the woman less than five minutes to dress, compose herself and meet me in the kitchen. Geez, I'm a mongrel!

It turns out that she had actually written on behalf of her sister and it was the sister who had driven out while we were getting organised. She'd taken off for the dentist so it was left to the letter writer to deal with us and the problem. Terrible when you get caught in your own trap.

The dog was a ripper with a real dislike for the whipper snipper and the vacuum cleaner. He was super smart though, so it didn't take too long to train this Ridgeback cross to do just what I wanted. The sister turned up just as we finished. Well timed, eh?

We've even stopped them in their own driveway. There's the client, wheeling out the wheelie bin when we spot her.

'Quick Bridge, go and grab her.'

Bridget the producer is out of the car in a flash. Straight up to the poor lady who by now is intent on climbing behind the wheel of her car. Now I've got to take my hat off to this producer of mine. She kept this poor lady talking for a good five or six minutes about absolutely nothing while we raced round the back of the Land Cruiser. The camera was loaded, I was miked up, we were all set. The soundo and I sat on the tailgate, and Rosie gunned the wagon straight up to the front of the woman's car. Brigitte did a rapid exit to the left and I strolled up, camera behind, casual as you like.

'G'day,' I say.

Geez, she nearly vaulted out of the car.

It's funny what people do the moment they realise they're trapped. Suddenly they're looking at everything. The kitchen's in disarray. The bed's unmade. The garbage tin's brimming over and all of this is going to be on television!! Oh my goodness. You can see them go into a mad mental panic. What do I move first? Sorry lady. You can't move anything. It's called continuity. Everything has got to look just the same as when we walked in the front door. Well, that's our excuse anyway. No you can't change, no you can't do your hair, no you can't put on some lippy. I want you just the way you are. The dog likes you doesn't he. And I like it too. Natural people, in their natural environment, are what this segment is all about. For me, it's my favourite part of the show. And it always will be. So if you've written us a letter and you get an unexpected knock on that front door of yours, don't be surprised when you open it if some bloke with a cap and spectacles smiles at you and says, 'G'day, I'm Doctor Harry.'

33

Animal Anomalies

These days nearly three-quarters of the letters, faxes and emails that arrive at our office each week speak of problems with animal behaviour. It really is only the last ten or fifteen years that have seen a real specialisation in this particular field of veterinary science. And it isn't just dogs and cats. It's all animals: birds, horses, and wild things as well. My visits to people whose animals are maladjusted to say the least are amusing, distressing and sometimes downright perplexing. Some probems are easily solved.

'My cat Tibby keeps drinking out of the toilet,' writes one viewer. To analyse a situation like this requires some thought and of course a house call. Tibby is your average moggy. A nice little tortoiseshell. Perhaps a fraction overweight, and certainly overindulged by her mum. It's incredible how animals start to look like their owners. Or is it vice versa? I never quite know. Anyway, we start by analysing Tibby's history. She seems to have had a pretty stable upbringing. Nothing untoward has happened to this poor feline, which could present as a pathological problem. Could I witness her current 'anti-social' behaviour? Not a worry. Sure enough, once you open the door, in goes Tibby and drinks merrily from the toilet bowl. This is a case of not only examining the cat, but the toilet as well. No blue in this loo. Drinks out of the shower as well. Goodness me. Nothing really wrong with situations like this. It's a return to primitive behaviour patterns where animals like to drink from pools in rocks and from running streams. The shower and the toilet are probably the closest things the cat can find to her natural environment. On top of all this, the water is lovely and cold as well.

'But how do I stop it?'

'Pretty easy,' I said. 'Why don't you close the toilet lid and the shower screen?'

Goodness me. Never thought of that.

'And give 'er a nice ceramic or terracotta bowl in the kitchen,' I added, 'and you'll never have another moment's worry.'

Toilets really do hold a fascination for a lot of animals, and for children too, don't they? Think back to your own youngsters. You're out visiting some long lost friend and just as the conversation gets to the interesting stage someone just has to go to the toilet. Kids love to check out any new water closet just in case it's different to the one at home. Thank heavens that in time the fascination wears off or life would be pretty tedious. Anyhow, back to the animals and this fox terrier who seemed to enjoy having a conversation with the toilet seat.

My father, as I've already mentioned, had bred fox terriers for many years. I can remember dog shows in my early childhood with seemingly hundreds of black and white or tan and white terriers, all barking, quivering and generally very much on edge. Nothing seems to have changed since. They're still pretty highly tuned dogs and I seem to find they're pretty well represented as a breed when it comes to unusual behaviours. This wretched foxie would fly through the house the moment the back door was opened. Straight into the toilet and he'd immediately start barking at the toilet lid—which of course answered back, because the dog kept knocking it up and down with his nose.

'Bark bark.'

'Clackety clack.'

'Bark, bark, bark.'

'Clickety clack, clack.'

Two minutes of this routine in a room with acoustics that amplify every little sound a hundred times would send you balmy, let alone deaf. The dog was off his tree. The more the toilet seat clattered, the more he barked at it, so the more it clattered. I put my foot on the damn thing—the seat, not the dog. All was silent. You wouldn't believe it. I put it up. Ah. But he'd seen that trick before. Down they came, lid and seat. And he was into it with even more gusto. Strike me lucky. It was worse than the front seat at a rock concert. What do you do with a dog like this? Probably not much. Just never buy another one. And they assured me that would be the case.

It was the toilet we had to attack. I took the seat and lid off and put them on the floor, next to the toilet. Enter the dog. Worried look on his face. Couldn't seem to realise that I'd just put it on the floor. Went round and round the toilet. No seat, no lid, no-one to talk to. So he didn't. Problem fixed. Well sort of. I'm glad it wasn't my toilet. I'm not a miracle worker. But this was not the end for the toilet terrier.

Out in the backyard he was just as bad. Anything that moved had to be attacked—and attacked with gusto. You couldn't sweep the pavement, dig in the garden, hose the lawn or perform any normal household task without this fruit-loop of a dog trying to grab hold of whatever you had in your hand and attempt to demolish it. Very hard to treat. He simply had a fetish for anything that moved. Only solution for this fella was to lock him up whenever you wanted to do anything!

Then there was the dog that liked to talk underwater. A lot of people tell me that this is something I can do—usually with a mouth full of marbles. But this dog really could. He was a cocker spaniel. Enough said. Great dogs, but hard to get beauty and brains in the one animal. We've got Cavaliers. They're pretty much the same. Cloth-headed, but love you to pieces. Back to the cocker. It seems that this dog used to get pretty distressed when the family went for a swim in their pool. Ooh, I had to see this. Sure enough, in they went, but not the dog. It ran frantically from one corner to the other, plunging its whole head into the water. I thought it was drinking. No way. The damn dog was barking—and barking underwater.

There were more nutty dogs per square inch in that area of Australia than I've ever encountered. Dogs that chased shadows, dogs that ripped washing off lines, dogs that tunnelled, and dogs that cringed.

Then there was the Doberman that didn't like the garage door. A couple of 'experts' had been to have a look at the situation. It's the remote control, that's the problem; it's the frequency of the waves from the controller to the door that make him bark. We can't hear 'em, but the dog can. No, no, it's not that at all, it's the noise of the door going up and down. That's what it is. We'll need to change that.

Interesting theories, I thought. Let's see what the dog does. As soon as you activate the door, the dog gets agitated. Soon as you get in the car, the dog gets worse. Move the car, and things become really intense. Okay. Let's try a few things. Let's take the dog out of the garage and let's play with the controller, right near the dog's ears. Dog looks at us like we're all stupid. Cancel theory number one. Let's put the dog in the car. Let's send the door up and down. Dog's as happy as Larry. Cancel theory number two. So what's the problem? This dog just loves his mum. When mum gets in the car and puts the door up, he knows from experience that he's going to be left behind. And he doesn't want that. He wants to be with mum. It's that simple. We call this separation anxiety—this great big Doberman, and he was a super terrific dog, loved his mum so much he couldn't bear to have her out of his sight. Some training, a bit of medication and a dog as smart as a Doberman will handle that problem, no trouble at all.

Separation anxiety can be a real problem for some dogs. And very often it is little dogs that tend to suffer worst. Take for instance a little toy poodle. This young man would spend all day every day with his family. He ate, drank and slept with them. Went out in the car and was always right under their feet wherever they were. Try going for a swim in the pool and see what happens. Sure enough the dog joins in too. It wouldn't be too bad if he just did laps, but he was more intent on getting as close as he could to whoever seemed to be making the most noise and then climbing all over them. Instead of being a pleasure, swimming became a chore. And people emerged from the pool covered in bright red scratch marks from the dog's claws. This curly black demon was despatched to Gran's house as the only possible way of controlling the problem.

These days birds too are starting to present problems. Parrots are the worst. I remember well this pink and grey galah. Boy, was he a nutter of the first order. He was originally bought and reared by a young lady with whom he spent most of the day. She would even take him to work. Indeed the relationship was so close that she would feed the bird by chewing up some of her own food and feeding him from her lips. This is courtship behaviour in so many birds, and it served to greatly intensify the bond between the two.

One of the biggest problems with birds is what we call imprinting. Young birds reared without contact with other birds of the same species become so closely bonded to the person caring for them that they may in fact imitate their every move. This can make for such a close bond between man (or woman) and bird that it becomes nearly impossible to break.

Such was the relationship between this lady and her bird. Time went by and eventually this young lady formed another relationship—and it wasn't with a bird. The galah of course took an instant dislike to this new light in her life. He went quite feral. Anytime the bloke appeared in the room or the bird heard his voice all hell would break loose. It would scream and scream as only galahs can! The bloke would have to go. That's when I first met Pinkie.

'You just have to do something,' pleaded Pinkie's owner.

Boy was this a challenge. With time and a fair bit of drug therapy we did finally manage to get Pinkie to at least allow the two of them to be together in the same room as he was, but he was only happy when he could see his mistress. All other contact had to be in another room, outside the house or in the pitch dark. After some twelve months I really did think we'd won. Pinkie was on his best behaviour and would even condescend to take a special treat from his mistress's fiance.

It was only a fortnight after their marriage that Pinkie arrived for another counselling session. Boy what a mess. This bird had really popped his cork. He was spending nearly the whole day with his head tucked under his wing, and only brought it out to go into a screaming frenzy.

'What on earth happened? I thought everything was going so well.'

'So did we,' the young lady said. 'We had just moved into our new house and decided to got out for tea to celebrate. Rob forgot the key and when we got home we were locked out.'

'Go on.'

'Well, we had no idea what to do but then I remembered I'd left the laundry window open a bit so Pinkie could have some fresh air. Rob got a ladder from the shed and climbed up, opened the laundry window and crawled in.'

'Yes.' The story was sounding pretty normal so far.

'Well, he was halfway in when he slipped and fell, right on top of Pinkie's cage. It was knocked over and he got a terrible fright.'

At this stage I knew for sure it was Pinkie she was referring to, not husband Rob. Let's face it, she'd known the bird for much longer. She went on to describe the bird's reaction. He went absolutely ballistic. Screamed, and screamed, and screamed. They ended up locking him up in the garage to get some peace.

This poor bird had lost it well and truly. I'm certain he

thought this intruder who he had just become accustomed to was intent on tearing him apart and he responded as any bird would when under fear of attack. His trust was gone. And it never returned.

What about the guinea fowl that thought it was a dog. There we are, up at Gympie, and what a great time to go. Floods everywhere. On our way up, the highway was cut in two places. I rang my wife to let her know I might not be back for a week. In spite of everything we got there, found the address, got some props for the shoot and sallied forth to surprise another Queenslander. Wringing wet she answered the door and soon I was confronted by a rather elegant guinea fowl who was obviously seriously attached to their blue cattle dog. It didn't matter where the dog went, there was the bird. And if for a minute the bird lost sight of the dog it would go into overdrive and squawk and carry on as only a guinea fowl can.

This bird had been reared with dogs and was of course imprinted on them. He may even have thought he was a dog! The solution was to expose this mixed-up bird to some of his own breed. Two mirrors, facing each other. Suddenly one guinea fowl became about forty! Brought him back to earth with a bit of a flutter.

But birds don't always like dogs. Picture the cockatiel. He's been mum's little man for at least three years. Sits on her shoulder the whole day. Their association is very close. Enter a young puppy. Suddenly mum's attention is split two ways. The dog and the bird have to share her time. Boy, is the bird's nose, sorry beak, out of joint. What does he do? Just what most birds would. He starts ripping his feathers out! Why birds seem to go for this approach has always baffled me. But there he sat on top of the curtain rod merrily plucking out feather after feather.

It's not easy to repair the damage. Birds on the whole are not as forgiving as dogs. A lot of time and effort and some medication to help things along is required, and we don't expect overnight results. As far as birds are concerned these relationships are very deep. In their eyes it is going to be a long road back before trust and confidence is restored. Don't laugh, it's absolutely true!

It takes time, patience and a good history to try to work out just what is going on in some of these situations. We don't always get it right. But you've got to try. The whole approach to managing behavioural problems in all animals is constantly being upgraded and in time I'm certain we'll be much better equipped to deal with any number of difficulties than we are at present.

A Tribute to Rosie, 1988-2000

Our dog Rosie died today,
And I was so very far away.
Sadly she died so all alone,
No-one to weep and none to moan.

My wonderful wife kissed Rosie goodbye;
She said, 'Animals know when they're going to die.'
Liver cancer we cannot cure
And who would want Rosie that pain to endure.

I'm sorry old girl, I couldn't be there,
But I guess you know I've shed many a tear.
In life you are torn in so many ways:
Work, home, family, it's truly a maze.

Border Collies, they are workers too;
And Rosie I've got work to do.
Though not in paddocks of fresh green grass;
My line of work's in a different class.

Often far away from our little farm,
Where life seems peaceful and mostly calm,
I've gone to the city with its smoke and grime,
Making television most of the time.

Yet you were always there when I came back,
With a wag of your tail and a quiet little yap.
That look in those eyes that says 'I need you',
Well, you know old friend, I needed you too.

A TRIBUTE TO ROSIE

Thanks for the hours we spent out walking,
You'd do the listening and I'd do the talking,
Across the flats and down through the creek,
We used to do it, nearly three times a week.

Thanks for that look from those dark brown eyes,
That stroke of the paw, those soft echoed sighs,
Thanks for your help with the sheep when 'twas needed,
You were great in the yards, and my voice always heeded.

Those big Suffolk rams were your greatest delight
And for all of their size you'd win any fight.
Old girl, you'd get cranky and your hackles would show,
A quick bite on the nose and they'd know where to go.

Often chasing after rabbits, I know you caught a few;
In days when you were younger, they ne'er eluded you.
But of late you'd grown slower, though still you'd do your best.
It was often one of your mates who would show a bit more zest.

Rosie, it doesn't matter, in fact you know it never did,
We loved you from the time you were just a little kid.
For who rates dogs on what they may or, it seems, they may not do?
That tangle with a stallion really put the wind up you.

Eleven years we've lived in Tassie, you came here as a pup.
You travelled down beside me on the front seat of a truck.
It was one of life's great journeys and you helped us see it through.
Then eight hundred stupid Polwarths, old girl we needed you.

The kennel's empty, no more growling at the possums after dark.
Your friends will yelp their loud 'hello', no more your happy bark.
Rosie, people often ask me if heaven's where good dogs go;
My answer is I pray they do, but one day we'll all know.

I'll be home on Saturday, and you'll be laid to rest,
In that very special garden, along with all the best.
For you, old girl, we'll find a place that catches all the sun,
That overlooks the paddocks where once you used to run.

A TRIBUTE TO ROSIE

Everyone called you Rosie, but often I called you Rose,
For you had all the sweetness of the sweetest flower that grows.
So a special rose we'll plant for you, or maybe two, or three,
Their perfume and the breezes will make perfect harmony.

I'll walk beside the garden and you know I'll give a call
To help me with some rounding up before the night should fall.
I'll feel your nose upon my hand, your tail against my thigh.
That touch for just a moment, then you know I'll cry.

Oh Rosie, my mate, you've done so much to help us through the years.
When times were tough, dogs understand, they see right past our tears.
When you get there, if we can help, just send the message through.
Though you'll be right, your good mate Pix, will be waiting there for you.

Rosie we miss you, all your friends miss you. You have gone
to join little Pixie (Pix, Heidi's little Cavalier King Charles
Spaniel, passed away nearly three years ago), so you won't
be on your own.

Rosie know this: every person on this earth who has ever
lost a dog shares our grief. 'Harry's Practice' will never be
the same for me, or for the millions who watch it. Thanks
Rose, thanks for being just the way you were, thanks for
being our dog and our friend. You will never be forgotten,
memories are something that not even time can take away.
Goodbye Rosie, goodbye.

*Janine, Heidi, Harry, and your canine friends, Chantelle,
Star, Misty, Cherie, Pepper, Belle, Cara, Ebony, Scarlet and
Isabelle.*